# Federal Elections

# Other Books in the Current Controversies series

# Federal Elections

*Debra A. Miller, Book Editor*

**GREENHAVEN PRESS**
*A part of Gale, Cengage Learning*

GALE
CENGAGE Learning

Detroit • New York • San Francisco • New Haven, Conn • Waterville, Maine • London

GALE
CENGAGE Learning

Christine Nasso, *Publisher*
Elizabeth Des Chenes, *Managing Editor*

© 2010 Greenhaven Press, a part of Gale, Cengage Learning

Gale and Greenhaven Press are registered trademarks used herein under license.

*For more information, contact:*
Greenhaven Press
27500 Drake Rd.
Farmington Hills, MI 48331-3535
Or you can visit our Internet site at gale.cengage.com

For product information and technology assistance, contact us at

Gale Customer Support, 1-800-877-4253
For permission to use material from this text or product, submit all requests online at www.cengage.com/permissions

Further permissions questions can be emailed to permissionrequest@cengage.com

Articles in Greenhaven Press anthologies are often edited for length to meet page requirements. In addition, original titles of these works are changed to clearly present the main thesis and to explicitly indicate the author's opinion. Every effort is made to ensure that Greenhaven Press accurately reflects the original intent of the authors. Every effort has been made to trace the owners of copyrighted material.

Cover image © Kim Kulish/Documentary Value/Corbis.

**LIBRARY OF CONGRESS CATALOGING-IN-PUBLICATION DATA**

Federal elections / Debra A. Miller, Book Editor.
    p. cm. -- (Current controversies)
    Includes bibliographical references and index.
    ISBN 978-0-7377-4705-8 (hardcover) -- ISBN 978-0-7377-4706-5 (pbk.)
    1. Elections--United States. 2. Election law--United States. 3. Electronic voting-- United States. I. Miller, Debra A.
    JK1976.F43 2010
    324.60973--dc22

                                                      2009038629

Printed in the United States of America
2 3 4 5 6 7 13 12 11 10

# Contents

## Chapter 1: Are There Serious Problems with the U.S. Federal Elections System?

**Yes: There Are Serious Problems with the U.S. Federal Elections System.**

## No: There Are No Serious Problems with the U.S. Federal Elections System.

## Chapter 2: Can Electronic Voting Technology Be Trusted?

Touch-screen electronic voting machines have caused controversy because of accuracy and security concerns, but there may be ways to correct these problems. In any case, voting systems are only one part of the overall problem of uncounted votes.

## Yes: Electronic Voting Technology Can Be Trusted

## No: Electronic Voting Technology Cannot Be Trusted

## Chapter 4: How Should the U.S. Elections System Be Reformed?

# Foreword

By definition, controversies are "discussions of questions in which opposing opinions clash" (*Webster's Twentieth Century Dictionary Unabridged*). Few would deny that controversies are a pervasive part of the human condition and exist on virtually every level of human enterprise. Controversies transpire between individuals and among groups, within nations and between nations. Controversies supply the grist necessary for progress by providing challenges and challengers to the status quo. They also create atmospheres where strife and warfare can flourish. A world without controversies would be a peaceful world; but it also would be, by and large, static and prosaic.

## The Series' Purpose

The purpose of the *Current Controversies* series is to explore many of the social, political, and economic controversies dominating the national and international scenes today. Titles selected for inclusion in the series are highly focused and specific. For example, from the larger category of criminal justice, *Current Controversies* deals with specific topics such as police brutality, gun control, white collar crime, and others. The debates in *Current Controversies* also are presented in a useful, timeless fashion. Articles and book excerpts included in each title are selected if they contribute valuable, long-range ideas to the overall debate. And wherever possible, current information is enhanced with historical documents and other relevant materials. Thus, while individual titles are current in focus, every effort is made to ensure that they will not become quickly outdated. Books in the *Current Controversies* series will remain important resources for librarians, teachers, and students for many years.

In addition to keeping the titles focused and specific, great care is taken in the editorial format of each book in the series. Book introductions and chapter prefaces are offered to provide background material for readers. Chapters are organized around several key questions that are answered with diverse opinions representing all points on the political spectrum. Materials in each chapter include opinions in which authors clearly disagree as well as alternative opinions in which authors may agree on a broader issue but disagree on the possible solutions. In this way, the content of each volume in *Current Controversies* mirrors the mosaic of opinions encountered in society. Readers will quickly realize that there are many viable answers to these complex issues. By questioning each author's conclusions, students and casual readers can begin to develop the critical thinking skills so important to evaluating opinionated material.

*Current Controversies* is also ideal for controlled research. Each anthology in the series is composed of primary sources taken from a wide gamut of informational categories including periodicals, newspapers, books, U.S. and foreign government documents, and the publications of private and public organizations. Readers will find factual support for reports, debates, and research papers covering all areas of important issues. In addition, an annotated table of contents, an index, a book and periodical bibliography, and a list of organizations to contact are included in each book to expedite further research.

Perhaps more than ever before in history, people are confronted with diverse and contradictory information. During the Persian Gulf War, for example, the public was not only treated to minute-to-minute coverage of the war, it was also inundated with critiques of the coverage and countless analyses of the factors motivating U.S. involvement. Being able to sort through the plethora of opinions accompanying today's major issues, and to draw one's own conclusions, can be a complicated and frustrating struggle. It is the editors' hope that *Current Controversies* will help readers with this struggle.

# Introduction

"*The U.S. Constitution sets up the basic system but allows the states to regulate most of the practical aspects of federal elections.*"

In the United States, voters elect officials to serve in three different levels of government—local, state, and federal— but it is through federal-level elections that national leaders such as the U.S. president and members of the U.S. Senate and U.S. House of Representatives are chosen. This system of federal elections in America is a dual system, governed by both federal and state laws. The U.S. Constitution sets up the basic system but allows the states to regulate most of the practical aspects of federal elections. However, the states are subject to several federal laws that have been enacted over the years to improve the election process.

The U.S. Constitution is the starting place for understanding the federal election system. Article II provides that the president and the vice president be elected together every four years and the Twenty-second Amendment limits their service to two terms. The Constitution also provides that the U.S. Senate has one hundred members, two from each state, elected for six-year terms. Members of the U.S. House of Representatives, however, are elected for two-year terms, and the number of representatives allotted to each state is based on the number of congressional districts in each state, which in turn is based roughly on each state's population. As of 2009, the House of Representatives has 435 members. These constitutional requirements result in simultaneous congressional and presidential elections every four years, with intervening congressional elections every two years—often called the midterm elections. Other constitutional provisions stipulate the qualifications for the presidency, vice presidency, and members of Congress; set the legal age of voting; prohibit discrimination based on race, color, or sex; and proscribe poll taxes that once required voters to pay for the right to vote.

Perhaps the most striking feature of the constitutional federal election system, however, is the electoral college. Although the Constitution provides that members of Congress be elected directly, based on the number of votes cast by the voters in each state, Article II sets up a separate, indirect election process for the presidency. Under this electoral college plan, each state appoints a number of electors based on the total number of senators and representatives to which the state is entitled, and these electors' votes then determine who is elected president and vice president, rather than the voters themselves.

In recent years, the electoral college system has been criticized, because, although rare, it is possible for a candidate to win the electoral vote, but lose the nationwide popular vote. In fact, this very situation occurred in 2000, when Republican candidate George W. Bush became president based on electoral college votes even though Democratic candidate Al Gore narrowly won the popular vote. Critics of the electoral college system claim it is inherently undemocratic and that it causes candidates to pay more attention to bigger states that have more electoral votes and certain highly competitive states whose votes can swing an election, neglecting voters in smaller and less competitive states. Defenders of the electoral college system point out that the nation's founding fathers created it as a check on majority or mob rule, and in order to give smaller states more influence in the presidential election. Despite this controversy, most experts do not expect the electoral college system to be abolished, largely because such a fundamental change would require a constitutional amendment and ratification by three-fourths of state legislatures.

The Constitution leaves many other aspects of federal elections—such as voter eligibility, registration, nominating processes, the operation of the electoral college, and the running of elections—up to the individual states. Perhaps not surprisingly, there are often differences among states on these issues. Some states, for example, prohibit those convicted of certain crimes from voting, either for a temporary period or permanently. State laws also differ on voter registration, with some states allowing citizens to register on the day of the election and others requiring advance registration. Many states also permit absentee voting—that is, voting by mail. Some of these states require a reason for absentee voting, such as disability, military service, or absence from the state, while others require no particular reason. States like California even provide for permanent absentee voter status, which automatically sends mail ballots to voters who have signed up as absentee voters. Many states that condone absentee voting also allow for early voting—that is, voting prior to the designated election date. States also decide on the controversial question of whether to use traditional paper ballots or electronic voting machines, and those that rely on paper ballots must decide how to count the votes—that is, whether to have humans do the counting or feed the ballots into electronic optical scanning devices to arrive at the total vote count.

Another important area in which states differ is how they nominate candidates for later presidential and congressional elections. Most states hold statewide primary elections for this purpose, although some primaries are closed (only members of each political party are permitted to vote for candidates representing their party), others are open (registered voters can vote in any party primary regardless of their political affiliation), and still others allow independent or unaffiliated voters to vote. However, fourteen states (Alaska, Colorado, Idaho, Kansas, Minnesota, North Dakota, Iowa, Nevada, Nebraska, Washington, Maine, Wyoming, Texas, Utah) do not hold primary elections but instead rely on a caucus system, in which interested and available voters personally attend a meeting to debate and decide on the candidate to represent their political party. States also set the date of their presidential primaries or caucuses—another issue that has caused controversy recently because a number of states have sought to hold their presidential primary elections early in order to gain more influence over the nominating process.

States have the final say in how the electoral college system works as well. Today, all states appoint electors based roughly on the popular vote—that is, voters in each state vote for the candidates of their choice, but in reality they are voting for a slate of electors who are designated by the candidates or political parties and pledged to vote for them. Most states ascribe to a winner-take-all system, in which the candidate who wins the most votes in the state receives all of that state's electoral votes. Two states, Maine and Nebraska, select electors based on both the statewide vote and the votes in each congressional district. There are a total of 538 electors nationwide, and the winner of the election is the candidate with the most (at least 270) electoral votes.

The federal elections system is further complicated by several federal laws designed to improve fairness in the voting process. In 1965, for example, Congress passed the Voting Rights Act to outlaw discriminatory state voting practices such as literacy tests, used to prevent African Americans from voting. Beginning in 1974, Congress enacted the Federal Election Campaign Act to provide public funding for presidential primaries and general elections and to require disclosure of private contributions to campaigns. This legislation has been amended several times to add other provisions and to create the Federal Election Commission, an agency that monitors federal campaign donations and spending. In 1986, the Uniformed and Overseas Citizens Absentee Voting Act required states to allow members of the armed services stationed overseas to cast absentee votes in federal elections. In 1993, the National Voter Registration Act forced states to make voter registration easier by allowing citizens to register at driver registration sites, schools, libraries, disability centers, and through the mail. In 2002, Congress passed the Help America Vote Act to allocate funds to states for the purchase of electronic voting machines. Finally, in 2002, Congress passed yet another campaign finance law—the Bipartisan Campaign Reform Act.

Despite improvements, the pros and cons of this complex system of federal elections continue to be debated. The authors of the viewpoints in *Current Controversies: Federal Elections* reflect the diversity of opinions about the country's federal elections system, offering their views on issues such as whether serious problems remain, whether electronic voting technology can be trusted, whether elections are fair, and what other reforms should be considered.

CHAPTER 1

# Are There Serious Problems with the U.S. Federal Elections System?

# Chapter Preface

The U.S. presidential election of 2000 produced one of the most divisive election crises in American history. The Democratic presidential nominee was former vice president Al Gore and the Republican presidential candidate was George W. Bush, then-governor of Texas and the son of former president George H.W. Bush. As the election approached, the race between the two candidates tightened, with no certain winner. In the end, Bush carried much of the South, the Midwest, and the Rocky Mountain region, as well as Ohio, Indiana, and Alaska, while Gore won most states in the Northeast, the Upper Midwest, the Pacific region, and Hawaii. Gore won the nationwide popular vote by close to 600,000 votes. When the electoral votes were counted, however, Bush was awarded 271 electoral votes with Gore winning only 266, giving Bush the presidency. The election was finally decided, however, only after a bitter controversy about which candidate actually won Florida's 25 electoral votes, in which a U.S. Supreme Court decision stopped a vote recount in Florida.

The nation's voters went to sleep on election night in the year 2000 without knowing who would be their next president. Early in the evening on election night, some television networks predicted, based on the results of exit polls in Florida, that Gore would be the winner, but these predictions were withdrawn after Bush seemed to be winning in the actual vote tallies. Around three in the morning, when it looked as if Bush had pulled ahead by about 50,000 votes, Gore even gave a concession speech, accepting defeat. By the morning after election day, however, Bush's lead in Florida had shrunk again. Gore was now ahead of Bush in electoral votes, but the results in three states—New Mexico, Oregon, and Florida—were still too close to call. Over the next few days, both New Mexico (5 electoral votes) and Oregon (7 electoral votes) were won by Gore, but the outcome in Florida, with its huge prize of 25 electoral votes, remained unclear. Since neither candidate had yet won enough electoral votes to win the election, Florida became the key to the presidency.

Over the next month, voters across the country watched a highly partisan legal scramble to claim the Florida votes. The final tally of votes in Florida showed Bush ahead, but only by about 300 votes. Gore therefore requested a hand recount of votes in four counties (Broward, Miami-Dade, Palm Beach, and Volusia), as provided for under Florida law. Florida secretary of state Katherine Harris, however, a staunch Republican and cochair of the state's Bush campaign, set a deadline of November 14 for completion of the recount—a deadline that three of the four counties (Broward, Palm Beach, and Miami-Dade) were unable to meet. At that point, secretary of state Harris and Florida governor Jeb Bush, George W. Bush's brother, certified George W. Bush as the winner by 537 votes. Gore quickly sued to protest the certification, and the Florida Supreme Court struck down the state certification for Bush and ordered a broad, statewide manual recount to begin.

Yet the Florida recount was ultimately blocked by the intervention of the U.S. Supreme Court in the dispute. The Court, on December 12, 2000, in a five-to-four decision written by conservative justice Antonin Scalia, ruled that the Florida court's plan for recounting ballots was unconstitutional, essentially because different standards could be applied by the people doing the recounts in different counties and precincts. The Supreme Court therefore reinstated the certification of George W. Bush as the winner of Florida's electoral votes—a decision that awarded him the presidency. Confronted with this decision, Gore conceded the election a second time, urging Americans to rally behind president-elect Bush.

The 2000 election marked the first time in the nation's history that a presidential election was decided by the Supreme Court and the second time that the winner of the electoral votes failed to win the national popular vote. It also led to continuing bitterness among large numbers of the public who suspected that Bush and his Republican supporters in Florida and on the U.S. Supreme Court essentially stole the election from Gore. These suspicions were heightened in 2001, when a study published by a Florida newspaper, the *St. Petersburg Times*, and supported by six major news companies—the *New York Times*, the *Wall Street Journal*, the *Washington Post*, the Tribune Company, the *Associated Press*, and CNN—found that Gore would have won if *all* uncounted ballots in Florida had been fairly counted. However, according to the study, Bush would have maintained a slight lead under the partial recount proposed by Gore or even the broader recount ordered by the Florida Supreme Court.

Finally, the election sparked a heated debate about various problems in the U.S. federal elections system that may have contributed to the bitter crisis in 2000. One of these issues involved paper punch-ballots and the difficulty of counting ballots when voters fail to follow instructions, do not punch completely through the ballot (which left "hanging chads" or bits of paper), or otherwise produced less-than-perfect indications of their voting choices. Largely in response to these problems, the U.S. Congress in 2002 passed the Help America Vote Act (HAVA), a law that provided funding to states to help them replace punch-card voting systems, established various minimum standards for the conduct of elections, and created the Election Assistance Commission to monitor and certify state voting procedures. HAVA encouraged many states to abandon paper ballots in favor of electronic voting machines, and, ironically, problems with these electronic voting machines have now created a new election controversy. The authors of the viewpoints in this chapter discuss this and other aspects of federal elections and debate whether serious problems remain in the federal elections system.

# Many Voters Faced Unacceptable Barriers to Voting in the 2008 Federal Elections

*Tova Andrea Wang*

*Tova Andrea Wang is a nationally known expert on election re-form and political participation and is vice president of research at Common Cause, where she focuses on voting rights, campaign finance, and media reform.*

Much has been made of the fact that there was no cata-strophic meltdown in the election system [in 2008]. The fact that problems were not as pervasive as they might have been is due to the hard work of the voting rights community and election administrators in the months and even years be-fore the election and the enthusiasm and persistence of voters. At the same time, thousands and thousands of voters faced unacceptable barriers to voting th[at] year, demonstrating that much more work remains to be done.

## Long Lines

While we are proud of the historic turnout on Election Day, the amount of time some Americans had to wait in order to vote was not just unfortunate, it could have denied the right to cast a ballot for many voters. While in many precincts, vot-ing took only a matter of minutes, in Detroit, some had to wait in line for five hours. In the St. Louis area it was six hours. In Chesapeake, VA, seven. Voters in Georgia and Florida faced unacceptably long wait times during early voting. While the commitment of so many to wait no matter how long it took was inspiring, some voters inevitably could not wait that long—they worked for hourly wages, couldn't get that much time off or had child care responsibilities.

Why were there such long lines? The data is insufficient to say with precision, but we do know some things. We knew going into the election that there was going to be much higher turnout than in the past, but that in many places, especially swing states [states without a consistent majority of Democrats or Republicans] where turnout would be highest, there were simply not going to be enough voting machines to handle the capacity. As we pointed out in our report on ten swing states, many states had no statewide standards on number of machines required per voter, while in other states, such as Virginia, the standard was inadequate. From another recent Common Cause report, we also know that machine breakdowns and problems with electronic poll books significantly exacerbated the problem of long waits, especially where there were insufficient backup plans.

---

*States with early voting had far less of a problem with long lines than states that did not.*

---

Other unnecessary confusion and controversy also likely added to wait times. For example, across the country, voters arrived at the polls to find they were not on the registration list. In some places there was confusion over what voter identification was required.

In the future, we need to put the resources and planning into our distribution and preparation of voting machines so that no one has to wait in line all day to exercise his right to vote. This means not only ensuring we have enough machines but also making sure that the plan for allocating those machines is based on a set of rational criteria and equity. For example, whereas Virginia law requires one voting machine for every 750 voters—and saw some of the worst of the lines—

Ohio had early voting and the Secretary of State directed that there be one machine for every 175 voters, and there were not, by and large, very long lines. We also need to make sure to have backup plans for when voting machines break down, which they do. Federal law should require that all precincts have stocked and utilize emergency paper ballots whenever any voting machine in a polling site goes down.

We also witnessed how much of a difference early voting can make. States with early voting had far less of a problem with long lines than states that did not. For example, North Carolina, which combined same day registration and early voting and had the biggest increase in turnout in the country, avoided this problem in most places on Election Day, whereas Pennsylvania did not. Unless and until Election Day can be run in such a way that it is easy and quick for all voters, all states should have a window of early voting. An effective early voting system is one that includes at least one weekend, has sufficient numbers of locations and equipment so that there are not unreasonable lines during early voting either, and early voting locations must be placed strategically in a way that best meets the needs of all voters.

*We need reform at the federal and state levels that not only criminalizes deceptive practices, but puts in place a mandatory procedure for law enforcement.*

## Deceptive Practices

[In the 2008 elections] we once again saw the insidious types of deceptive practices that are designed to suppress voting— misinformation campaigns meant to mislead and confuse voters about whether they can vote and how, when and where to vote. In the past, this had usually taken the form of flyers and mailings, but [in 2008], as we predicted in our deceptive practices report, such activities went online as well. We heard robocalls [prerecorded-message phone calls] spreading false information about voting, and we saw emails and text messages in Virginia, Missouri, Florida and at least five other states doing the same. Most of these emails said that given the high turnout expected, Republicans were to vote on Tuesday, Democrats on Wednesday. An email went to the entire student body of [Virginia's] George Mason University that appeared to be from the provost of the school making this same claim. There were robocalls in Florida and Nevada telling people they could vote by phone and calls in Virginia fraudulently telling people the wrong place to vote. In the days prior to the election there were emails in places like Texas and Florida with misleading information about straight ticket voting and voter identification rules. The Secretary of State of Ohio's website was hacked into in the days leading to the election, causing it to be shut down for several hours.

---

*Untold numbers of voters registered to vote but were not on the registration list when they came to vote and had to cast a provisional ballot.*

---

As always, there were the more traditional flyers in the Philadelphia area telling people if they had outstanding parking tickets or traffic violations they would be arrested at the polls. And a flyer was circulated in Virginia, again with the message that Republicans vote on Tuesday, Democrats on Wednesday. Although law enforcement caught the creator of this flyer, no charges were pressed as it was deemed to have been a "joke."

Currently, the Department of Justice does not believe there is a federal statute that explicitly criminalizes this activity. This needs to change. We need reform at the federal and state levels that not only criminalizes deceptive practices, but puts in place a mandatory procedure for law enforcement and election officials working with community and voting rights organizations to debunk the false information and disseminate the correct information rapidly. Law enforcement should also put in the energy and resources it needs to pursue the perpetrators. As we discussed in our deceptive practices report, there are already a number of laws on the books that could be used to go after the people responsible for these tactics, given a prosecutor with the will to do it.

## Registration

Issues around the voter registration process were the most controversial of th[at] election year. Untold numbers of voters registered to vote but were not on the registration list when they came to vote and had to cast a provisional ballot.

Across the country, there were overblown charges against ACORN [Association of Community Organizations for Reform Now] and other voter registration organizations regarding voter registration fraud. This led to Republican demands and litigation seeking the names and other information of all voters who had been registered by ACORN, such as in Pennsylvania, presumably so they could be investigated and/or challenged.

> *The government needs to take a more proactive role in [the voter registration] process so that we have in the end a system of universal registration.*

In Florida Secretary of State Kurt Browning insisted that the information on voters' registration forms exactly match the information in state and federal databases in order for that registration to be processed, even though we know that processing errors, typos, variations on names and the like constitute the overwhelming majority of "mismatches." This led to over 22,000 voters having their voter registration initially blocked. As of Election Day, some 10,000 of these voters had yet to take the extra, unnecessary step of resubmitting an ID, and their vote was thus in jeopardy. Similarly, the GOP

[Grand Old Party; i.e., the Republican Party] sued the Secretary of State of Ohio, demanding that 200,000 voters who had a discrepancy between their voter registration information and information in other databases be flagged and likely forced to vote provisionally. The Secretary of State in Georgia similarly flagged tens of thousands of voters and challenged the citizenship of thousands of eligible voters based on "mismatches." In Colorado, the Secretary of State rejected voter registration forms for picayune [trivial] technical omissions and was found by a federal judge to have purged voters from the rolls in violation of federal law.

All of these incidents underscore the need to completely rethink how we do voter registration in this country, unique in that it places almost the entire burden on citizens to register to vote and make sure they stay registered throughout their lives.

---

*The specter of "caging"—challenging prospective voters'*
*right to vote—arose once again [in the 2008 elections].*

---

The government needs to take a more pro-active role in this process so that we have in the end a system of universal registration. This means the expansion of same day registration from nine states to all 50. Once again, the states with the highest turnout were states such as Minnesota, Wisconsin, Iowa and North Carolina, which all allow eligible citizens to register to vote on Election Day. North Carolina instituted Election Day registration [in 2008] during early voting for the first time, and had the biggest increase in turnout in the country. We should also institute pre-registration of 16- and 17-year-olds in high school and automatic registration of citizens who interface with the government in any number of ways, including with Departments of Motor Vehicles (DMV), public assistance agencies, and upon completion of a term of incarceration and finalization of the naturalization process.

Elections officials could update registrations of existing voters whenever they move within state based upon data readily available from U.S. Postal Service change of address databases, DMV databases, the Civil Service board, Social Security, Medicare, Medicaid, and state and federal income tax databases. Citizens would receive notices that their registration would be automatically updated to their new location unless they responded, to provide for those who may not wish to change their registrations, such as college students or those in the military who are only temporarily relocating and wish to vote at the permanent address.

## Caging and Challenges

Early on in the fall [2008] election season, state Republican officials were reportedly planning on using lists of people whose homes had been foreclosed as a basis for mounting challenges to their right to vote at the polls. In Michigan, this led to the Democratic Party suing for an injunction prohibiting challenges on the basis of being in foreclosure. In Ohio and other states, election administrators sent out directives and statements that foreclosure was not a legitimate basis for a challenge. The Montana Republican Party challenged the eligibility of 6,000 registered voters in six counties that historically are Democratic strongholds. A lawsuit by the state Democratic Party forced the Republicans to shut the operation down.

In addition, as noted, the allegations regarding fraudulent and "nonmatch" registration forms led to serious concerns that the lists of those who had discrepancies or were registered through a third party organization would be challenged at the polls.

In addition, the specter of "caging"—challenging prospective voters' right to vote—arose once again. In Ohio, a state law that required election administrators to send out a mailing to all voters 60 days in advance of the election raised concerns that those pieces of mail that were returned as undeliverable would be used as a basis for challenges—a practice that had been utilized repeatedly over the last 40 years. Secretary [Jennifer] Brunner issued a directive that a piece of undeliverable mail could not be the sole basis for a challenge. In Florida, Democrats brought a lawsuit asking the court to clarify what types of challenges were legitimate because of information they had that Republicans in that state were engaged in caging.

That caging and challenges declined in 2008 compared to 2004 is a testament to the publicity that voting rights advocates have brought to the perniciousness of the process, and a result of the pre-election litigation victories voting rights lawyers had [achieved] to prevent it. Nonetheless, the fear of caging and challenges to voting rights should no longer be part and parcel of every election as it has been since the 1960s.

We need federal legislation banning caging, such as the bill introduced in the United States Senate. The proposed Caging Prohibition Act prohibits challenges to a person's eligibility to register or vote based solely on returned mail or a caging list, and mandates that anyone who challenges another person's right to vote must set forth the specific grounds for their alleged ineligibility, based on first-hand knowledge, under penalty of perjury.

---

*"Voter registration fraud" while problematic and illegal, does not lead to vote fraud at the polls. It never has.*

---

In addition, states must establish fair standards for challenges. All states should have uniform challenge procedures characterized by transparency and fairness; such procedures must be designed in a way that prevents disenfranchisement or voter deterrence. On Election Day, only poll workers should have the legal authority to challenge a voter—not another voter or a poll watcher. States should enact stringent requirements for when someone can make a challenge at the polls, and the bases upon which such challenges can be made must be narrowly defined. Such challenges should be based on personal knowledge and documentary evidence of lack of eligibility. States should also require pre-election challenges to be filed well ahead of Election Day, and similarly be based on very particularized charges and on personal knowledge and/or documentary evidence. The Justice Department should also actively pursue vote caging and polling place challenges clearly based on race or ethnicity.

## Mickey Mouse Did Not Vote

In states across the country, Republicans charged the community organizing and voter registration organization ACORN of massive voter registration fraud. The [John] McCain campaign for a period of time made this a centerpiece of its stump speeches. The campaign charged the organization was a criminal enterprise and threatened to destroy the fabric of democracy. As has been well documented, these charges were overblown. During this tumult, voting advocates repeatedly reminded the public that "voter registration fraud" while problematic and illegal, does not lead to vote fraud at the polls. It never has. This episode was just another in the continuing effort of some to lead the American people to believe that there is massive voting fraud in this country when there is not, in order to pass restrictions and erect unnecessary barriers to voting.

Once again, in the days now passed since Election Day [2008], there has not been a single charge, not a single allegation of fraud at the polling place. As predicted, the name Mickey Mouse might have appeared on a registration form because someone was too lazy to do the hard work of voter registration, but Mickey Mouse never made it on to the official voter rolls and of course he DID NOT VOTE. Despite all the usual overheated rhetoric about the potential for massive vote fraud, none of this has materialized.

This underscores the need to continue to fight barriers to voting that are premised on false charges of vote fraud, such as strict voter identification requirements and requiring proof of citizenship in order to register to vote. Increasingly states have been passing such measures and we can expect that to continue in [ensuing years]. Such laws are wholly unnecessary and serve only to disenfranchise, especially minorities, young people, the elderly, the poor and people with disabilities. This was demonstrated [on] Election Day [2008] in places like Indiana, which has the strictest identification law in the country, where students were turned away at the polls because they lacked the proper identification.

---

*The effort to make our system one in which every American citizen is able to easily vote and have his vote counted is far from over.*

---

The truth is, if this election had been much closer, the outcry over the problems enumerated would be huge. If, for example, the presidential election had hinged on Indiana, where it was extremely close, there would have been microscopic inspection of that state's election system and problems undoubtedly revealed. Litigation would likely have ensued. We dodged that bullet. But that does not mean our great democracy is everything it should be. The effort to make our system one in which every American citizen is able to easily vote and have his vote counted is far from over.

# Problems with New Electronic Voting Machines Were Manifold in the 2008 Elections

*Steven Rosenfeld*

*Steven Rosenfeld is a senior fellow at Alternet, an online news-wire, and author of the book* Count My Vote: A Citizen's Guide to Voting.

The electronic voting problems in the 2008 election are broader than recently-publicized snafus such as machines not turning on, voter databases omitting names, or touch screens not properly recording votes, according to an analysis of 1,700 incident reports from the nation's largest voter hotline.

Moreover, the voting machine issues and the confusion they caused among poll workers appear to have compounded the delays faced by untold thousands of voters [in 2008], a preliminary analysis of 1-8[66]-OUR-VOTE reports by Joseph Lorenzo Hall, a researcher at Princeton University and the University of California, has found.

"If we can do anything to improve the experience of the average voter facing a machine problem, it should be reduce the amount of time they spend in line," Hall wrote [in November 2008], adding that voters who had machine problems and got back-up paper ballots often were not confident that their votes would count.

"Another curious feature of the data is the voters' uniformly negative attitudes toward contingency or back-up plans," he said. "Voters are often upset and mistrustful."

Hall's analysis is one of the first assessments to look at electronic voting in the 2008 fall election. Many voting rights

groups have said the biggest problems th[at] year were inaccurate voter registration records, not enough early voting sites,
and planning that did not accommodate high turnout. Hall's
findings suggest that the voting machinery used exacerbated
these very issues.

---

*The most common voter hotline complaints were "about
broken machinery, long lines, long waits to vote and reports of emergency ballots being used."*

---

## Hundreds of Incident Reports

During early voting and on Election Day [2008], the Election
Protection Coalition, which had a volunteer staff of 10,000
lawyers, received calls via a national hotline, 1-866-OUR-
VOTE. The calls were notated, categorized and posted on
OurVoteLive.org. Of 86,000 calls received, about 1,900—or 2.2
percent—were about the machines. Two-thirds were registration and polling place inquiries.

There were 1,700 incidents after eliminating duplicates,
Hall said. These calls generally did not involve problems encountered later Tuesday night during the vote count, he said
in an e-mail. In contrast, the Democratic National Committee's
election protection team monitoring machine issues, including
the count, recorded "thousands" of incidents, a volunteer on
that team said.

The most common voter hotline complaints were "about
broken machinery, long lines, long waits to vote and reports
of emergency ballots being used instead of the normal mode
of voting," Hall said. "However, there are some interesting features from these reports."

Machine breakdowns and electronic poll book bottle-
necks—where voters check in before voting—lead to many
delays, Hall said. He cited a report from Atlanta where all 15
voting machines in a polling place had stopped working, and

a New York City report of one poll book for hundreds of voters. A shortage of e-poll book laptops was reported in Georgia, while in Maryland poll workers could not get their electronic voting systems up and running, he said, citing typical complaints.

One surprise, Hall said, was that the delays in voting did not just come with checking in voters—but with voters wanting to run their ballots through vote-count scanners. "We have reports of people waiting in line for 3 hours in New Jersey, 3.5 hours in Georgia, 5 hours in Ohio, 6 hours in Missouri," he said. "In many cases, long lines were exacerbated by voters insisting on feeding their own ballot into an optical scan machine, despite it taking a long time to service or replace the affected equipment."

Hall said he was "very encouraged to see that in most cases, emergency ballots were available," though he noted that in Virginia some precincts ran out of backup ballots. "What I didn't count on was that voters consider voting via an emergency ballot to be fundamentally suspect; that is, most were worried that their vote wouldn't count if cast via emergency ballot."

---

*Machinery-related problems are more extensive than many people assume.*

---

Poll workers compounded this issue, he said, by confusing backup and provisional ballots. The latter are used for unlisted voters and must be verified to count.

"We saw cases in at least two states where poll workers were refusing to hand out emergency ballots despite significant machine failures," he said, referring to New York and Pennsylvania. "In one case a caller claimed that voters in line were 'fighting with poll workers' over emergency ballots," he said. In addition, some voters were upset their vote was not secret because election officials could see their backup ballots.

It is impossible to know how many votes were affected by the issues cited in these incident reports. However, depending on the state and location, individual paperless voting machines could be used by 200 to 600 voters, and paper-ballot scanners could be used to count even larger numbers of ballots. While the presidential results would not appear to be undermined by any of these problems, they do reveal that machinery-related problems are more extensive than many people assume.

## Machinery Still Unfamiliar

Hall's report noted other categories of voting machine issues. Since 2002, federal law has encouraged the use of paperless voting systems, especially for people with disabilities. However, Hall said "disability access equipment simply didn't work or was not set up properly" in Arizona, California, New York, Missouri, Minnesota and Maryland. He also noted a report of a poll worker not helping a blind voter because too many other voters were in line.

Machinery malfunctions were a common complaint, Hall said, saying New Jersey and Pennsylvania experienced "numerous reports of lights and buttons not working on machines." In addition, he said there were reports of machines that kept rebooting, "would work only after periodic shaking," or did not work with other computers in the network.

---

*The process of paperless voting . . . confused some voters.*

---

In 14 states, voters reported "vote flipping," where the machines selected another candidate other than their pick.

Voters raised the issue of who was authorized to fix broken machines. In South Carolina, "individuals removed a voting machine from the polling place and took it out to a car to tinker with it," Hall said. In New York, others, including a policeman, apparently "fixed" voting machines. Voters in Ohio and Pennsylvania also noted clocks on some machines were still set to Daylight Savings time, which prompted them to question whether their votes would count.

The process of paperless voting also confused some voters. "A 'fleeing voter' is a voter who leaves a voting machine without having cast their voted ballot," he said, citing incident reports from New Jersey, New York and Pennsylvania where that was an issue. "A 'premature voter' is one who accidentally casts their ballot (or has it cast for them) before they are finished voting their ballot," Hall said, citing reports from Ohio, Pennsylvania, Virginia, Florida and Chicago.

Straight-party voting or selecting candidates from one political party also had glitches, he said. In some instances, not all the candidates were selected, as in Washington, D.C. In Virginia and Pennsylvania, there were reports of ballots where the presidential race "was the only contest available," or the opposite, where the presidential race "was the only race missing."

Computer scanners that read paper ballots had other problems. Reports from Ohio, Virginia, Minnesota, Texas and North Carolina found counters on scanners did not record when new ballots were inserted, an issue that raised concerns about vote count accuracy. In Ohio, Missouri, Illinois and California, printers attached to paperless voting machines to create a paper record of electronic votes failed. In Virginia, scanners could not read wet or humid paper ballots. In Florida and California, using the wrong kind of pen caused votes to be misread, the incident reports said.

Poll workers also were confused with how to handle backup paper ballots, Hall said. In California, New York and Pennsylvania, it was not clear where to put these ballots after people voted, he said. Some security seals on boxes were broken, he said, and in some cases ballots were "just laying around" or "stacked on top of machines," as was the case in Minnesota.

"In a few cases, poll workers intentionally or mistakenly cast a voter's ballot before they are finished voting or before they've had a chance to revise their ballot," Hall said, citing examples from New York, Virginia, Illinois and Arizona.

# Frontloading the Primary System Has Reduced Meaningful Voter Participation

*Lonna Rae Atkeson and Cherie D. Maestas*

*Lonna Rae Atkeson is a professor and Regents' Lecturer in the Political Science Department at the University of New Mexico. Cherie D. Maestas is an associate professor in the Political Science Department at Florida State University.*

[A] significant feature of the [presidential] nomination process that affects meaningful participation [by voters] is the timing of the state-level events. States select the dates of their nomination contests independently, though party rules provide some guidelines, and states have incentives to schedule them early. The collective result has been an increasingly frontloaded nomination calendar with many states vying to hold primaries early in the season. Frontloading began in earnest in 1988 and has continued to increase. Frontloading, in fact, was seen as so important in 2008 that two states moved their nominating events to dates where they were openly defying national party rules. . . . In 1976, the primary season was largely drawn out with less than 50% of primaries conducted half way through the time period, and this same pattern holds for all competitive early primaries prior to 1988. In 1988, however, frontloading is quite evident, with more than 50% of primaries conducted by week seven. The 2008 pattern shows an even greater rise in the number of primaries completed quickly.

## Changes from Frontloading

Frontloading is a tremendous change to the electoral context in the sequential system of delegate selection. The compression of the primary system influences candidate behavior and ultimately voter behavior. Frontloading has led to an increase in the importance of events in the invisible primary and the advantage given to the frontrunner and it has increased the problem of information to the voter.

Perhaps the most important way that frontloading influences participation is by determining the eventual nominee earlier in the process, leaving many voters to participate in a fictional contest of preferences when the outcome of the race is already known. As a result, frontloading enhances the importance of the earliest contests and reduces the importance of later contests. This happens because delegates accumulate more quickly for the eventual winner and because the race winnows more quickly. The forces of momentum send clear signals of viability to voters and campaign donors, so many candidates expend the bulk of their resources quickly in the hopes that a big win will propel their candidacy to the next set of nominating events. Candidates withdraw more quickly when their campaigns run out of steam because they are not anointed with "big mo" [momentum].

---

*The increasing trend to declare the winner quickly affects the type of campaign to which voters in different states are exposed.*

---

Prior to frontloading, candidates stayed in the race much longer, creating a larger field for voters to consider and providing greater incentives for voters across the electorate to tune in and participate in the selection of their party's nominee. In 1972 for example, nine Democratic candidates ran for the party nomination and by the end of the nomination season two-thirds of them remained. In comparison, in 1988 only two Democratic candidates out of seven remained during the entire delegate selection period; and for Republicans only the eventual nominee was left over two months before the delegate-selection process ended. By 2000 both parties effectively ended their campaigns almost three months before the last primary was held; and, in the Republican Party, at least half the field withdrew before the first delegate selection event was conducted. . . .

The increasing trend to declare the winner quickly affects the type of campaign to which voters in different states are exposed. In the earliest states, voters see a full slate of candidates, intense campaigning, and a disproportionate share of media attention. This is because early contests are important to momentum and for the most part candidates place all their campaign chips in the earliest contests. The concentration on advertising in these states reflects candidates' needs to perform better than expected in the first few primaries to stimulate momentum for future races. Not surprisingly, the media responds to the intense campaigning early in the process with almost constant coverage in early races, but a dropoff in coverage quickly occurs as the campaign events become less important to the nomination outcome.

> [Frontloading] privileges voters in some states and penalizes those in others, thereby failing to meet the goal of encouraging broad [voter] participation.

Two other aspects of frontloading are worth considering because they also affect the context of the campaigns to which voters are exposed. The first is that frontloading increases primary compression, leading to a larger number of contests on any given day. For example, in 2008 the Democrats opened up their window of participation on February 5, resulting in Tsunami Tuesday with the largest number of contests ever held on one day. Compression is problematic for candidate strategy because candidates must divide their campaign dollars among numerous states at the same time. Because candidates court different constituencies, each candidate makes different strategic decisions resulting in very different primary contests across states. These differences include different levels of competition, mobilization, and information for nomination participants. These strategic choices result in different levels of turnout and judgments across electorates. We argue that these factors undermine meaningful participation.

The second is that frontloading often leads to separation of the presidential nomination contest from other nomination contests in the state. In the era before frontloading was prevalent (pre-1988), most states combined their state and federal ballots. After frontloading, however, a majority of states held their presidential primaries on a different date than their state primaries. Placing both elections on the same day enhances voter interest as more races are on the ballot and more candidates across races actively compete. The separation of these contests reduces turnout and functionally reduces the meaningful participation of primary voters in presidential and state politics.

Does the frontloaded system that has evolved since the reforms meet the goals of meaningful participation as sought by reformers? We think not. The current incentive structure privileges voters in some states and penalizes those in others, thereby failing to meet the goal of encouraging broad participation. In the earliest states, voters are exposed to an intense multi-candidate contest, where their decisions are seen as the harbinger of the campaign. Because the race is new and every candidate has a chance to win the nomination (at least in theory), votes in these states "count" more. The outcomes from early state contests provide important cues to future voters about the viability and electability of candidates, and can breathe life and the all-important momentum into the underdog campaign. As each subsequent election takes place, however, the dynamics of the campaign change: the field is winnowed, candidates cease campaigning, the "cues" from any one state become less important to future states, and media attention wanes.

Once the winner of the nomination has been declared voters in remaining states lack meaningful choices at the polls. Without the prodding that an active campaign provides and because whatever marginal effect voters' choices would make to an election outcome is lost when the candidate is known, voters have fewer incentives to participate. It is not surprising to find that state primary turnout declines in states that fall late in the sequence of contests. Estimates from an empirical model suggests that between 3.5 to 7% (or between 71,000 and 178,000 voters) per state are turned off by their position in the process and their lack of meaningful participation.

## The 2008 Election

There is no doubt that the 2008 Democratic contest was one of the most dramatic and drawn-out nominations contests in recent times, and the level of participation was greater than in previous elections. Does this mean that frontloading is not an impediment to broad participation? Probably it is not. First, frontloading certainly influenced the Republican race in the way we describe above, by winnowing the field to a single viable candidate quite quickly after Tsunami Tuesday. The winner-take-all delegate counts piled up rapidly for McCain and, although Huckabee stayed in the race until March 4, the race was effectively over after Romney suspended his campaign on February 7. Nineteen primaries still remained.

---

*Even in the 2008 [presidential] contest ... frontloading was consequential to the outcome.*

---

Although the Democrat race winnowed to two candidates quickly, the two candidates remained in a competitive contest to the end of the process. But, the oddities of this race likely make it unique. For example, the status of Michigan and Florida delegates were unclear until a party deal was brokered at the end of the process. As early states in the process, they should have provided momentum to the winning candidate going into Tsunami Tuesday, but the degree to which a win in those states mattered was unclear. Subsequent primary voters were left with confusing signals about momentum. That meant that voters went into Tsunami Tuesday with no clear frontrunner from the earlier contests and the short distance between contests left little time for voters to deliberate their choices. Instead the vote-share differences across races were relatively small and there were two state wins for senators Barack Obama and Hillary Clinton, and the rest of the field, except John Edwards, who was hanging on by a thread, had conceded. This, combined with rules that proportionally allocated delegates, and candidates' strategic targeting of resources on Tsunami Tuesday, led to an extremely close split in delegate counts and state wins in what became a two-person contest. The renewed competitiveness of the election and the full campaign coffers of Obama and Clinton created a highly unusual circumstance never seen before and led to an uptick in turnout and a renewed enthusiasm and interest in the campaign. Given that this is one very unusual contest out of 20 since the reforms, it appears to be the odd case out and is not reflective of normal nomination politics.

That being said, it may highlight an important problem in frontloading never considered before because compression had never been as intense as it was on Tsunami Tuesday 2008. Specifically, it suggests that if there is not enough time for momentum to signal to voters the frontrunner, a compressed schedule might actually exacerbate competition and party divisiveness because of candidate strategies, creating a drawn out, but not necessarily meaningful battle. Thus, in this scenario, voters do not have clear signals from previous voters, nor do they have the full campaign to respond to because of candidate incentives to target their campaigning efforts and because of the speed of the process.

Thus, even in the 2008 contest we argue that frontloading was consequential to the outcome. Extreme compression in the race led candidates to employ selective mobilization efforts. Obama concentrated his efforts on the states holding caucuses while ceding some key primary states to Clinton, and Clinton focused on primary elections rather than caucuses. One problem with frontloading is that compression forces candidates to strategically select where to compete and this has consequences for the participation of state electorates. States where one candidate strategically cedes the race and skips campaigning generate less effective participation. Rank-and-file party members are not drawn into the race in the same way they would be in a state where both candidates choose to compete. This means that outcomes are less reflective of the underlying rank-and-file preferences than if the nomination contests had been spread out over time, encouraging two competitive candidates to focus on the same state. The result was an aggregate outcome that increased overall participation throughout the process, but with uneven mobilization of underlying electorates in individual states. Thus, although frontloading did not stymie broad participation in this case, it likely created biases in participation in individual state electorates due to selective state targeting by candidates. . . .

## Reducing Meaningful Participation

[The frontloaded system] has consequences on candidate and voter behavior that reduces meaningful participation. Voters in the earliest states experience a very different campaign with active candidates and media coverage leading to the necessary information to make an informed choice. In addition, voters in these states are in the unique position that a vote for even a losing candidate may send important information about their viability to later voters. Thus, these voters have relatively high voting incentives and low voting costs, leading to more meaningful participation and an increased likelihood of turnout than later voters. Up to the effective end of the campaign, each subsequent primary has lower turnout as the prospects of the frontrunner increase and the incentives to turn out in support of a likely loser decrease. Also, once the nominee is known, participation rates sharply decline since candidates no longer have the incentives to stimulate participation and voters no longer have incentives to participate.

---

*The current system does not offer meaningful participation to all or even most voters.*

---

This result is problematic in the face of a reformed process that was intended to enhance internal party democracy and to promote meaningful and fair participation across all states, particularly for groups that were typically underrepresented in the process. Mobilization efforts in competitive elections have an especially strong effect on young voters, less-educated voters, and low-income voters. Therefore, it is likely that a frontloaded, sequential nomination process in which mobilization efforts cease before all states have selected a nominee creates a disproportionate burden on some classes of voters.

Recent discussions by political elites, party leaders, and political pundits also question the sanity and effectiveness of the nomination process as it has evolved, particularly as it relates to frontloading and its consequences. Political pundit David Broder argues that the rapid succession of numerous state primaries may result in the inability of voters to make a quality and deliberative decision given the choices offered. Simply, there is not enough time between state contests for voters to make a well-informed choice. Party leaders have expressed similar concerns. . . .

All this suggests that the current system does not offer meaningful participation to all or even most voters. Some voters' participation is more meaningful than others and their judgments are more important in selecting the party nominee.

# The Caucus System Is Undemocratic

*Julia Tagliere*

*Julia Tagliere is a former educator who now works as a writer, editor, and translator.*

I can still remember the day I voted for the first time. I had spent almost my entire seventeenth year being drilled by my mother about how voting was my civic responsibility; how our founding fathers, suffragettes, and succeeding generations of brave and patriotic souls had sacrificed so much to guarantee me that right; how the identity of the candidate for whom I voted was private, and that I never had to share that information with anyone. It was such a thrilling leadup to that moment when I stepped up and used the stylus to punch through that first ballot card. My mother and I went out to lunch together afterwards to celebrate; it was a wonderful, memorable day.

Many years and many elections have passed since that day, and I have voted in each and every one. Would I say I'm a political activist? No; I don't post signs in my yard, I don't put stickers on my car, I don't campaign for anyone, and I don't make financial contributions to any parties or candidates. My sole political activism comes, and always has come, from exercising that precious right to have my vote be counted. It was a right I took for granted right up until the day I moved from Illinois, a state which uses the primary system to choose candidates for presidential elections, to a new state, Minnesota, which uses the caucus system.

## Introduction to the Caucus

Until I moved, I had no real concept of what a caucus was. All I really knew was that those crazy people in Iowa had them all the time, and that it was a big deal because, so everyone said, they were often pretty good predictors of who the final candidates would turn out to be in the general election. Some part of me just assumed, when I moved, that a caucus would be conducted in essentially the same fashion as the primaries had been back in Illinois: you study the issues and the candidates' positions; you register to vote; you get a card telling you where to go; you show up, mark your ballot, and get a little sticker that says, "I Voted Today," hooray for me! How wrong I was.

As I began to read more articles about the upcoming caucuses in the local papers, I grew more and more concerned that perhaps I was ill-informed about the caucus process, so I visited my party's website. It mentioned a lot about selecting delegates and discussing possible additions to the existing party platforms, but didn't really answer my key question, which was "How do I vote in a caucus?"

Seeking further clarification, I called our local party headquarters, reasoning that I could get clearer answers from a live human being. I did, but they were answers I found to be extremely disappointing. My first disappointment was that a caucus isn't like a primary election at all. It's more like a town hall meeting, where caucus goers show up and spend two hours doing just what the website said they do: they talk about selecting delegates to the next level of caucus and discuss any desired additions to the existing party platforms.

"Okay," I said to the representative on the other end of the line, "So when do we vote?"

"Well, you don't really vote in a caucus. After all of the other items on the agenda have been covered, people might want to discuss or debate a little bit, and then there's a straw poll to divide the caucus up into groups by their favored candidate. You know, there'd be a McCain group, a Huckabee group, a Romney group . . ." Divide into groups? How is that a secret ballot?

The representative might have gone on a lot longer than that if I'd let him, but I was still stuck way back on his first statement: "You don't really vote in a caucus." I was so stuck on that, that in fact, I asked him to repeat it twice, to make sure I'd heard him correctly.

"So let me get this straight: I show up to a meeting, talk about the issues, about which I'm already comfortable I've made up my mind, select the delegates, and then there's a straw poll, and this whole process is going to take two and a half hours." Having spent most of my adult life in the Chicago area, time factors are always a concern for me.

"Well, if you show up, say, around seven-thirty or eight o'clock, that's probably pretty close to when the straw poll would happen, so if you time it just right, yeah, you could be out of there more quickly."

"Okay, so I show up right on time, cast my straw poll vote, and then I leave, and my vote gets counted."

"Not exactly."

What the 'not exactly' means, I discovered after further probing, was that even if I did manage to split the seconds properly and get there just in time to place a vote for the candidate of my choice, that didn't necessarily mean that the delegates selected by the group earlier in the meeting have to go to the convention and vote for that particular candidate (an excellent incentive to take part in the delegate-selection process, I guess). The fog was starting to lift, and I was not enjoying the view.

"So let me get this straight: I could show up, cast my straw poll vote, leave, then the delegate goes to the convention and decides he or she doesn't want to vote for my candidate, so my vote means nothing?"

"Not exactly." What that 'not exactly' means is that Minnesota's Super Tuesday caucus is only the beginning for Minnesota voters, and ultimately, it may have little to do with the party's final choice for candidate (remember, Minnesota went for Romney). Once the precinct caucuses have been held, then there are county or district-level conventions, which the chosen precinct delegates attend. After that, there is the congressional district convention. Then, according to *The Minnesota Monitor*, "In Minnesota, each of the state's eight congressional districts select three delegates for the convention. These are pledged delegates and will have a presidential preference attached to their voting at the national convention. Each congressional district chooses how that presidential preference will be allocated. At the state convention, another fourteen at-large delegates are chosen who may or may not be bound by presidential preference. That decision is made by a vote of the convention attendees."

---

*In the early 1830s, the country . . . realized that allowing a select number of meeting attendees to decide who the candidate would be . . . gave those attendees too much power.*

---

"So really," I asked my, by now, exasperated representative, "my vote at the caucus Super Tuesday does not really count for anything except choosing a delegate, who may or may not wind up actually selecting the candidate for whom I have indicated a preference?"

"Yeah, I guess if you look at it like that, but you do still get to state a preference."

"But I don't want to state a preference! I want to vote! When do I get to vote?"

Clearly, the representative did not understand my concerns, any more than I understood how a caucus was a better system than the primary one I had been taking for granted. It's true that, initially, at least, the caucus was the system of choice used by our country to select candidates for presidential office, but in the early 1830s, the country began to come to its senses and realized that allowing a select number of meeting attendees to decide who the candidate would be, rather than allowing people to vote for themselves, gave those attendees too much power, and could actually be seen as an "undemocratic" way of doing things. Today, of the fifty states, just fourteen currently use the caucus system; the rest have decided to let all of the voters have a say, not just those voters who choose to or are able to attend a meeting; in this fashion, primary states avoid widespread disenfranchisement of the voting population.

---

*[In 2008] the already-restrictive structure of the caucus system imploded under . . . crushing and demanding voter turnout for both parties.*

---

## Implosion of the Caucus System in 2008

On Super Tuesday in Minnesota [in 2008], the true effect of the caucus system as it currently operates was not "democracy in action," which many supporters of the caucus system spout off as the true "beauty" of the system; rather, the real effect of this arcane and convoluted system was the true disenfranchisement of thousands of people statewide.

Normally, caucuses only take place for just two and a half hours on one single night. In Illinois, and other states where primary systems are in place, the polls are open all day, to allow people the opportunity to vote. The Minnesota caucus system penalizes those who work night shifts, those who are unable to attend meetings due to illness or disability, college students in classes—it even penalizes those who are out of the state on caucus night, as the system makes no allowance for absentee ballots. None.

Normally, just due to those factors alone, there would be a large number of voters in the state who simply cannot participate because of the logistical barriers imposed by this archaic system. But [in 2008], the already-restrictive structure of the caucus system imploded under the weight of an issue one would have thought to be every "Rock the Vote" advocate's dream: crushing and demanding voter turnout for both parties.

If Minnesota had had a primary system, this would not have been a problem that caused thousands of people to be disenfranchised. But because of the limited hours of the caucus, the lengthy discussions taking place, the general sense of confusion about the process itself, and the inability of volunteers to address the needs of such a large turnout, there were problems galore.

The morning after the caucus, there were vociferous complaints about traffic jams, parking problems, location confusion, and long lines, and those were just the beginning. Some precincts actually ran out of ballots and wound up indicating their preferences (note how I do not say 'votes') on Post-It notes or cut-up slips of paper. Other precincts were so overwhelmed that they closed their doors a full hour ahead of time, cutting the time for this beautiful "democracy in action" experience to just an hour and a half.

What happened to all of those people waiting in line? What happened to all of those people stuck in traffic jams, unable even to approach their caucus site? What happened to all of those people circling neighborhoods trying to find a parking place? What happened? I'll tell you what happened. They were disenfranchised. There is no way to get around that. The system failed to give these voters their rightful opportunity to express their vote, and it is time for this system to change.

## Support for Change

The two major political parties in Minnesota, the DFL [Democratic-Farmer-Labor] and the Republican Party, both experienced difficulties on caucus night, the DFL more so than the Republicans, and that fact was reflected in the party reactions to voter complaints in the days following the caucus. The DFL Party, which claimed more than 200,000 caucus goers, immediately led a charge calling for a switch to a primary system, spearheaded by Senators Ann Rest and Linda Scheid. Their proposed bill would "allow voters to participate in a primary similar to a general election without requiring them to be involved in the caucus process now run by political parties." DFL chairman Brian Melendez echoed those sentiments, saying that "switching to a presidential primary—while keeping the caucuses for other races and for party governance—is worth talking about." That's more like it!

But just as my hopes began to inch up for the restoration of sanity to my newly adopted state's "preference declaration" system, I read the Republican Party's response to the proposal. GOP [Grand Old Party, a nickname for the Republican Party] Chairman Ron Carey said that he and other party leaders resolutely oppose "any change from our caucus system." He also, in a very flattering comment for diehard caucus lovers, stated that he believed that if Minnesota were to separate a primary from the caucus system, then "the only people who [would] show up for the caucuses would be the true insiders and geeks."

It is worthwhile to note, at this point, that the GOP turnout for the caucuses, while still enormous, numbered a mere 60,000, compared to the 200,000 racked up by those lovable DFLers. With an inflexible and disrespectful attitude such as Carey's, those numbers cannot be mere coincidence. And yet, even with that record-breaking turnout, in a state with a population of roughly 5.2 million, that is still fewer than 300,000 people who were able to exercise their sacred right to "express a presidential preference," a number that does not even come close to being truly representative of the "voice of the people."

Isn't low voter turnout something that both parties should still be concerned about, even in th[at] year of "record-breaking" turnout? Let's face it, it's not hard to break a record if you're setting the bar low enough. The voice of the people spoke loudly and clearly in the aftermath of the precinct caucuses here in Minnesota on Super Tuesday; it said "Stop the caucus! I want to get off!"

So why isn't this need for change being supported by both parties? Easy: old habits die hard. Minnesota does it this way, because that's the way, with one brief, shining period of exception back in 1992, that Minnesota has done it since 1959. Prior to that year, interestingly enough, Minnesota was actually the first state to create a statewide primary system. The switch to a caucus system is nowadays blamed on primary upsets suffered by the two major parties during Dwight Eisenhower's campaign, and later during Estes Kefauver's.

---

*Switch back to a primary and give me back my vote.*

---

So there was an upset! Upsets happen all the time—did New England decide not to participate in any future Super Bowls because they were upset by the New York Giants? In the end, no system is perfect, to be sure. But at least with a primary, all are welcome, and, here's the key: all are made to feel welcome.

When I expressed my concerns to the party representative—that I didn't know if I could make it to my caucus location within the time allotted, that I thought it was really exclusionary the way the caucus system was set up in Minnesota, that I really felt I was in danger of being disenfranchised—his response was not even remotely sympathetic:

"Gee, I'm sorry you feel that way. Welcome to Minnesota, and thank you for calling your Republican Party headquarters. Is there anything else I can help you with?" . . .

My vote is my activism. So yes, there is something else my representative can help me with: switch back to a primary and give me back my vote.

# The 2006 Midterm Elections Restored Voters' Trust in U.S. Voting Devices

*Ben Arnoldy and Ari Pinkus*

*Ben Arnoldy and Ari Pinkus are staff writers for the* Christian Science Monitor, *an international daily newspaper.*

This week [November 7, 2006], American democracy let out a collective sigh of relief.

Young voters took part in record numbers, despite growing up during one of the most troubled eras of American voting. Some 1.2 million poll workers minded the details and, for the most part, avoided election-altering gaffes. In precincts where problems did pop up, some voters got the word out through amateur videos; others waited in lines in a silent testament that the day wasn't a pointless exercise.

In the end, exit polls found 88 percent of respondents felt confident in their voting device that day. And the widespread concerns about the legitimacy of recent elections didn't discourage more than 40 percent of registered voters from showing up—apparently, the highest midterm turnout in a generation. "Decision 2006" may be remembered as a confidence-restoring election.

"We've seen more change in the past six years than we've seen in the previous 200" in the technology of voting, says Paul DeGregorio, chairman of the Election Assistance Commission, charged with assisting federal reforms. "I think we're going to see more change, and certainly the introduction of more technology in this election process because people seem to like it and it works well."

---

*The consensus among election observers is that the problems . . . appeared to be isolated and not systemic.*

---

## Election Glitches

The election was far from smooth, however. Among the glitches:

- Machine problems. Some didn't start up, others displayed the wrong ballot, and others, according to unverified allegations, registered votes for candidates whom voters had not picked.

- Poll worker gaffes. In several states, voters reported being asked for unnecessary identification. In Montana, a worker forgot to reset a counter, delaying the tally.

- Allegations of voter suppression. Democrats in New Mexico have charged that voters received calls that offered directions to the wrong polling place. In Virginia, the FBI is investigating similar complaints as well as an allegation that a resident was threatened with arrest if he voted.

But the consensus among election observers is that the problems—while still too numerous for comfort and difficult to track with some electronic voting technologies—appeared to be isolated and not systemic.

"In 2006, there were more problems overall, but they were largely minor," says Doug Chapin, director of electionline.org, a nonpartisan reform watchdog in Washington. "Lots of fender benders, no pileups."

The problems weren't surprising, he and others say, in a year that saw the largest rollout ever of electronic voting machines. More than 4 in 5 voters used some kind of electronic ballot [in 2006].

"In lots of jurisdictions, preparation kept them from having any major problems," says Mr. Chapin, who lauded Connecticut in particular for "obsessive" planning. "In the places where they did have problems, they just got lucky that they weren't in races that ended up being close."

Money also helped. [In 2006], states spent the bulk of the $3.1 billion given out under the Help America Vote Act of 2002. Mr. DeGregorio says money went not just to equipment but to poll-worker recruitment and training as well as voter education.

The snags, he says, arose from inattention. "It shows that details matter in the conduct of elections [and] we can do a better job of helping to professionalize election administration in this country."

Intense scrutiny of the process has helped poll workers stay on their toes, say experts.

---

*Overall turnout surged to more than 40 percent [in 2006], its highest level in a midterm election since 1982.*

---

[In 2006], a new initiative called "Video the Vote" enlisted amateurs to film poll irregularities. The idea: to bring attention to voting problems even in elections where the winning margin was large enough that they would normally receive little attention.

"There's so much focus on calling the winners and losers ... that we lose sight of whether the voter was a winner or loser," says Ian Inaba, one of the leaders of the project that has posted hundreds of interviews at videothevote.org. "You look at those lines in Denver and Missouri or listen to some of those voters in Maryland or even New Jersey—things were not OK [on Election Day]. There were a lot of frustrated people."

Mr. Inaba and political bloggers are using more democratic media models to widen engagement in politics. They may be among many reasons that more people are checking back into politics.

## High Turnout

Overall turnout surged to more than 40 percent [in 2006], its highest level in a midterm election since 1982, according to a preliminary analysis by the Center for the Study of the American Electorate.

Several states saw gains over 2002, including Ohio, Montana, and Missouri, according to the Associated Press.

Hotly contested races in those states might have fueled the increases.

"Polarization tends to be a mobilizing factor in getting out the vote," says Peter Levine, director of CIRCLE, a voter-research institute at the University of Maryland.

The turnout of young people in [the 2006] election was especially strong.

Voters aged 18 to 29 cast an estimated 10 million votes, or 13 percent of all ballots, up from 11 percent in 2002.

In one crucial election, the Senate race in Montana, young people made up 17 percent of the vote. The winning campaign of Democrat Jon Tester said it made "fairly aggressive" efforts to reach that demographic.

"There's a new generation of voters that will turn out . . . if candidates target their vote. Young voters have left their mark on the 2006 election. It shows that they are a force," says Heather Smith of Young Voter Strategies, a nonpartisan organization in Washington aimed at increasing youth turnout.

Young people voted for Democrats by a wide margin: 22 percentage points, according to CNN's exit poll data. Many sought change on issues like Iraq, jobs, and education, says Celinda Lake, a Democratic pollster.

"The turnout shows that young people have confidence in the voting system," says Mr. Levine. In general, the millennial generation has more positive attitudes toward government institutions than people might expect, he adds.

Ultimately, perceptions of progress in election reform may rest on the orderly resolution of the Senate race in Virginia.

News agencies have declared Democrat James Webb the winner, but at press time election workers had yet to finish canvassing votes and the incumbent, Sen. George Allen (R), had not conceded. [Webb won—ed.]

Any recount would not scrutinize individual ballots but merely recheck tabulations. This is partly due to the state's switch to paperless electronic machines, a system widely criticized for the lack of transparency in just such an event.

# The Federal Election System Functioned Well in 2008

## The Pew Center on the States

*The Pew Center on the States identifies and advances state policy solutions and is part of the Pew Charitable Trusts, an independent nonprofit organization that seeks to improve public policy, inform the public, and stimulate civic life.*

A "meltdown scenario;" "historic" turnout; a system that "has never been taxed or burdened or used to [this] extent."

The predictions of what might happen when polls opened November 4 [2008] often relied on superlatives. The results might take days, some guessed, either because of delays in processing mail-in ballots, the need to count absentee and provisional ballots or the possibility of recounts in one or more states that could tip the balance in either direction for the White House and for other offices. Voters could endure endless lines. Provisional ballots could trigger post-election lawsuits as millions might have registration problems or lack proper ID.

Yet when clocks on the East Coast struck 11 p.m.—the moment polls closed in a number of West Coast states, including California, Oregon and Washington, we had a new president-elect by a wide Electoral College margin. We also discovered that our myriad election systems functioned well enough to restore some of the confidence that had been shaken in previous years.

The people spoke, and it appears the voting machines, tabulators and results accurately reflected their choices for president.

## Successes and Challenges

*Electionline*'s preview of the 2008 general election, released exactly two weeks before polls opened on November 4, was entitled "What If They Held an Election and Everyone Came?" Now, just over a month after, we have our first look at the results.

In this, the 23rd *electionline.org* briefing, the successes and challenges of the Nov. 4, 2008 election are examined. With predictions of huge turnout and chaos at the polls, why did the system in many parts of the country seem to manage so well? In cases where things did not go as well, why were voters left off the rolls? What challenges remain in election administration, nearly eight years after the 2000 vote that inspired wholesale change in the way Americans cast ballots? And does the substantial margin of victory for president mask problems that would be under the microscope if that margin were slimmer, as in 2000?

---

*Experts have credited convenience voting—both in-person early voting and no-excuse absentee voting—for a relatively smooth Election Day.*

---

Turnout predictions, based on early voting numbers as well as voter registrations, fell short of the record-breaking numbers.

Many accounts from Election Day indicate turnout was extremely high in the morning as polls opened and steady, if not light, through the rest of the day. When poll closing times approached, observers found it difficult to find almost any voters.

Experts have credited convenience voting—both in-person early voting and no-excuse absentee voting—for a relatively smooth Election Day.

Others have noted that turnout was actually depressed among Republicans, some of whom upon hearing tracking polls and early voting turnout figures, might have decided not to bother fighting the crowds and casting a ballot.

"The intensity was one sided," said Curtis Gans, director of the Center for the Study of the American Electorate. "It was on the Democrats' side."

---

*The numerous machines that make up the backbone of America's election system, while still evolving, mostly handled the challenge of a high turnout election.*

---

Still, about 130 million Americans cast ballots leading up to and on November 4, the most in the history of the United States. Approximately 61 percent of the voting-eligible population cast ballots, a modest increase over the 60 percent who cast ballots in 2004. It was the highest turnout since 1968.

More than 38 million ballots were cast before Election Day, either in person at early voting centers or through in-person or by-mail absentee voting.

The numerous machines that make up the backbone of America's election system, while still evolving, mostly handled the challenge of a high turnout election.

Machines, by most accounts, performed adequately. Optical-scan systems, introduced for the first time in a presidential election in South Florida, operated largely without a hitch. Electronic voting machines, vilified in some quarters as insecure, not auditable and unverifiable, were used throughout Georgia, Maryland, most of Texas and Pennsylvania and many other states. While some prepared for the worst (Pennsylvania had emergency ballots on hand anticipating the possibility of machine breakdowns) contingency plans were rarely employed.

## A Few Problems

There were problems in some areas. A few polling places in Allegheny County, Pa. had to use paper ballots when more than half of the electronic voting machines did not work. Ballot-on-demand printers, used at some Florida early voting locations, could not keep up with the work load, causing long lines at a few locations. The residual vote rate—the number of ballots for which a vote for president could not be counted—increased in six out of 10 states that released turnout figures along with unofficial vote counts. Residual votes more than doubled in Michigan (from .7 percent in 2004 to 1.8 percent in 2008), increased in South Dakota (from 1.7 percent in 2004 to 2.5 percent in 2008) and rose by lesser amounts in Minnesota, North Dakota, Florida and New Hampshire.

As the residual vote indicates, just like any human endeavor, Election Day is never perfect, and November 4 was no exception.

A national hotline established to collect, log and map voter complaints and concerns on Election Day received more than 200,000 calls, many of which focused on registration problems and machine concerns.

Campaigns were also on hand in battleground states, with armies of lawyers, canvassers, phone bank volunteers and polling-place locators.

The U.S. Department of Justice watched the polls as well, not only in states covered by the Voting Rights Act but Northeastern cities (Boston, New York City and Philadelphia) as well as parts of Ohio and Washington.

# Voter Turnout in the 2008 Presidential Election Hit a Forty-Year High

*Associated Press*

*The Associated Press is the largest and oldest news organization in the world, serving as a source of news, photos, graphics, audio, and video.*

Enthusiasm among blacks and Democrats for Barack Obama's candidacy pushed voter turnout in [the 2008] elections to the highest level in 40 years.

Final figures from nearly every state and the District of Columbia showed that more than 131 million people voted, the most ever for a presidential election. A little more than 122 million voted in 2004.

[The 2008] total is 61.6 percent of the nation's eligible voters, the highest turnout rate since 1968, when Republican Richard M. Nixon defeated Democrat Hubert Humphrey, said Michael McDonald, a political science professor at George Mason University.

States finished certifying their election results [the] weekend [after], including California on Saturday. The Electoral College was scheduled to elect Mr. Obama president on [the following] Monday, with electors meeting in each state to vote in a largely ceremonial procedure.

Turnout increased for the third straight presidential election, encouraging news for those who have warned about voter apathy. [In 2004], 60.1 percent of those eligible voted.

"We seem to have restored the levels of civic engagement that we had in the 1950s and 1960s," McDonald said. "But we didn't break those levels."

## Analysis of the Turnout

McDonald calculated turnout rates based on the number of eligible voters among adult U.S. citizens. Experts calculate turnout rates in different ways based on whom they consider eligible voters, a process that excludes noncitizens and, in most states, convicted felons.

---

*[Turnout] was . . . helped by a surge in black voters, who had the opportunity to elect the first black president.*

---

Regardless of the method, turnout fell short of many predictions, in part because voters in some Republican areas of the country were not as enthusiastic this year with Sen. John McCain as the party's nominee as they were [in 2004] when President Bush won a second term.

Mr. Bush's unpopularity after eight years in office, the nation's fatigue with the Iraq war and the worst economic crisis since the Great Depression—coupled with Mr. Obama's message of change—contributed to the increased turnout for Mr. Obama. He was also helped by a surge in black voters, who had the opportunity to elect the first black president.

The number of registered Democrats jumped in many states, helping to propel Mr. Obama to a larger share of the vote than Sen. John Kerry, the 2004 Democratic nominee, in 44 states and the District of Columbia.

Early voting hit a new high, with about 41 million people—or more than 31 percent—voting before Election Day, either by mail or at designated sites, according to returns compiled by the Associated Press. Early voting accounted for 22 percent of the votes cast in 2004.

The Obama campaign invested heavily in early voting, and it appeared to be the difference in several states, though many of those people might have eventually voted on Election Day.

Voter turnout increased substantially in newly competitive states such as Virginia, Indiana and North Carolina, which all went for Mr. Obama after decades of favoring Republican presidential candidates. Turnout also increased in some Republican states with large black populations, such as Mississippi, South Carolina and Georgia.

North Carolina, which had competitive elections for president, governor and Senate, had the biggest increase in turnout, from 57.8 percent in 2004 to 65.8 percent [in 2008].

"I don't know that we did anything different than in other states, but the magnitude was so different," said North Carolina Democratic Chairman Jerry Meek. "We were the only state in the country with a nationally targeted presidential race, gubernatorial race and Senate race."

Mr. Obama won North Carolina by 14,177 votes, out of more than 4.3 million cast. In the Senate race, Democrat Kay Hagan beat incumbent Republican Elizabeth Dole. Beverly Perdue was elected the state's first female governor.

Minnesota, with a competitive Senate race . . . , had the highest turnout rate, even though it dropped slightly, to 77.8 percent. It was followed by Wisconsin, Maine, New Hampshire and Iowa.

West Virginia and Hawaii tied for the lowest turnout rate, at 50.6 percent. Arkansas, Utah and Texas came close.

In all, the turnout rate increased in 33 states and the District of Columbia.

Turnout dropped in some states that did not have competitive presidential contests, such as Utah and Oregon. Oregon had been a battleground in previous presidential elections and the state had a competitive Senate race.

# CHAPTER 2

# Can Electronic Voting Technology Be Trusted?

# Chapter Overview

*Bruce Schneier*

*Bruce Schneier is an internationally renowned security technologist and author.*

In the aftermath of the American presidential election on 2 November 2004, electronic voting machines are again in the news. Computerised machines lost votes, subtracted votes, and doubled some votes too. And because many of these machines have no paper audit trails, a large number of votes will never be counted.

While it is unlikely that deliberate voting-machine fraud changed the result of this presidential election, the internet is buzzing with rumours and allegations in a number of different jurisdictions and races. It is still too early to tell if any of these problems affected any individual state's election. . . .

The US has been here before. After the 2000 election, voting-machine problems made international headlines. The government appropriated money to fix the problems nationwide. Unfortunately, electronic voting machines—although presented as the solution—have largely made the problem worse. This doesn't mean that these machines should be abandoned, but they need to be designed to increase both their accuracy, and people's trust in their accuracy.

This is difficult, but not impossible.

## Characteristics of a Good Voting System

Before I discuss electronic voting machines, I need to explain why voting is so difficult. In my view, a voting system has four required characteristics:

Bruce Schneier, "What's Wrong with Electronic Voting Machines?" *OpenDemocracy.net*, September 11, 2004. Copyright © Bruce Schneier. Published by openDemocracy Ltd. Reproduced by permission.

1. Accuracy. The goal of any voting system is to establish the intent of each individual voter, and translate those intents into a final tally. To the extent that a voting system fails to do this, it is undesirable. This characteristic also includes security: It should be impossible to change someone else's vote, stuff ballots, destroy votes, or otherwise affect the accuracy of the final tally.

2. Anonymity. Secret ballots are fundamental to democracy, and voting systems must be designed to facilitate voter anonymity.

3. Scalability. Voting systems need to be able to handle very large elections. Nearly 120 million people voted in the [2004] US presidential election. About 372 million people voted in India's May 2004 national elections, and over 115 million in Brazil's October 2004 local elections. The complexity of an election is another issue. Unlike in many countries where the national election is a single vote for a person or a party, a United States voter is faced with dozens of individual election decisions: national, local, and everything in between.

4. Speed. Voting systems should produce results quickly. This is particularly important in the United States, where people expect to learn the results of the day's election before bedtime.

Through the centuries, different technologies have done their best. Stones and potshards dropped in Greek vases gave way to paper ballots dropped in sealed boxes. Mechanical voting booths, punch-cards, and then optical scan machines replaced hand-counted ballots. New computerised voting machines promise even more efficiency, and internet voting even more convenience.

But in the rush to improve speed and scalability, accuracy has been sacrificed. And to reiterate: accuracy is not how well the ballots are counted by, say, a punch-card reader. It's not how the tabulating machine deals with hanging chads, pregnant chads, or anything like that. Accuracy is how well the process translates voter intent into appropriately counted votes.

## Trust a Computer to Be Inaccurate

Technology gets in the way of accuracy by adding steps. Each additional step means more potential errors, simply because no technology is perfect. Consider an optical-scan voting system. The voter fills in ovals on a piece of paper, which is fed into an optical-scan reader. The reader senses the filled-in ovals and tabulates the votes. This system has several steps: voter to ballot, to ovals, to optical reader, to vote tabulator, to centralised total.

At each step, errors can occur. If the ballot is confusing, some voters will fill in the wrong ovals. If a voter doesn't fill them in properly, or if the reader is malfunctioning, then the sensor won't sense the ovals properly. Mistakes in tabulation—either in the machine or when machine totals get aggregated into larger totals—also cause errors.

A manual system of tallying the ballots by hand, and then doing it again to double-check, is more accurate simply because there are fewer steps.

---

*In close races, errors can affect the outcome, and that's the point of a recount.*

---

The error rates in modern systems can be significant. Some voting technologies have a 5% error rate, which means one in twenty people who vote using the system don't have their votes counted. A system like this operates under the assumption that most of the time the errors don't matter. If you consider that the errors are uniformly distributed—in other

73

words, that they affect each candidate with equal probability—then they won't affect the final outcome except in very close races.

So we're willing to sacrifice accuracy to get a voting system that will handle large and complicated elections more quickly.

In close races, errors can affect the outcome, and that's the point of a recount. A recount is an alternate system of tabulating votes: one that is slower (because it's manual), simpler (because it just focuses on one race), and therefore more accurate.

Note that this is only true if everyone votes using the same machines. If parts of a town that tend to support candidate A use a voting system with a higher error rate than the voting system used in parts of town that tend to support candidate B, then the results will be skewed against candidate A.

## Touch-Screen Voting Machines

With this background, the problem with computerised voting machines becomes clear. Actually, "computerised voting machines" is a bad choice of words. Many of today's mechanical voting technologies involve computers too. Computers tabulate both punch-card and optical-scan machines.

---

*The very same software that makes touch-screen voting systems so friendly also makes them inaccurate in the worst possible way.*

---

The current debate centres on all-computer voting systems, primarily touch-screen systems, called Direct Record Electronic (DRE) machines (the voting system used in India's May 2004 election—a computer with a series of buttons—is subject to the same issues).

In these systems the voter is presented with a list of choices on a screen, perhaps multiple screens if there are multiple elections, and he indicates his choice by touching the screen.

As Daniel Tokaji points out, these machines are easy to use, produce final tallies immediately after the polls close, and can handle very complicated elections. They can also display instructions in different languages and allow for the blind or otherwise handicapped to vote without assistance.

They're also more error-prone. The very same software that makes touch-screen voting systems so friendly also makes them inaccurate in the worst possible way.

'Bugs' or errors in software are commonplace, as any computer user knows. Computer programs regularly malfunction, sometimes in surprising and subtle ways. This is true for all software, including the software in computerised voting machines.

For example:

In Fairfax County, Virginia in 2003, a programming error in the electronic-voting machines caused them to mysteriously subtract 100 votes from one candidate's totals.

In a 2003 election in Boone County, Iowa the electronic vote-counting equipment showed that more than 140,000 votes had been cast in the municipal elections, even though only half of the county's 50,000 residents were eligible to vote.

In San Bernardino County, California in 2001, a programming error caused the computer to look for votes in the wrong portion of the ballot in 33 local elections, which meant that no votes registered on those ballots for that election. A recount was done by hand.

In Volusia County, Florida in 2000, an electronic voting machine gave Al Gore a final vote count of negative 16,022 votes.

There are literally hundreds of similar stories.

What's important about these problems is not that they resulted in a less accurate tally, but that the errors were not uniformly distributed; they affected one candidate more than the other. This is evidence that you can't assume errors will cancel each other out; you have to assume that any error will skew the results significantly and affect the result of the election.

## Security

Another issue is that software can be 'hacked'. That is, someone can deliberately introduce an error that modifies the result in favour of his preferred candidate.

This has nothing to do with whether the voting machines are hooked up to the internet on election day, as Daniel Tokaji seems to believe. The threat is that the computer code could be modified while it is being developed and tested, either by one of the programmers or a hacker who gains access to the voting-machine company's network. It's much easier to surreptitiously modify a software system than a hardware system, and it's much easier to make these modifications undetectable.

Malicious changes or errors in the software can have far-reaching effects. A problem with a manual machine just affects that machine. A software problem, whether accidental or intentional, can affect many thousands of machines and skew the results of an entire election.

Some have argued in favour of touch-screen voting systems, citing the millions of dollars that are handled every day by ATMs and other computerised financial systems. That argument ignores another vital characteristic of voting systems: anonymity.

Computerised financial systems get most of their security from audit. If a problem is suspected, auditors can go back through the records of the system and figure out what happened. And if the problem turns out to be real, the transaction can be unwound and fixed. Because elections are anonymous, that kind of security just isn't possible.

None of this means that we should abandon touch-screen voting; the benefits of DRE machines are too great to throw away. But it does mean that we need to recognise the limitations, and design systems that can be accurate despite them.

## Solutions

Computer security experts are unanimous on what to do (some voting experts disagree, but it is the computer security experts who need to be listened to; the problems here are with the computer, not with the fact that the computer is being used in a voting application). They have two recommendations, echoed by [computer expert] Siva Vaidhyanathan:

1. DRE machines must have a voter-verifiable paper audit trails (sometimes called a voter-verified paper ballot). This is a paper ballot printed out by the voting machine, which the voter is allowed to look at and verify. He doesn't take it home with him. Either he looks at it on the machine behind a glass screen, or he takes the paper and puts it into a ballot box. The point of this is twofold: it allows the voter to confirm that his vote was recorded in the manner he intended, and it provides the mechanism for a recount if there are problems with the machine.

2. Software used on DRE machines must be open to public scrutiny. This also has two functions: it allows any interested party to examine the software and find bugs, which can then be corrected, a public analysis that improves security; and it increases public confidence in the voting process if the software is public, no one can insinuate that the voting system has unfairness built into the code (companies that make these machines regularly argue that they need to keep their software secret for security reasons. Don't believe them. In this instance, secrecy has nothing to do with security).

Computerised systems with these characteristics won't be perfect—no piece of software is—but they'll be much better than what we have now. We need to treat voting software like we treat any other high-reliability system.

The auditing that is conducted on slot machine software in the US is significantly more meticulous than that applied to voting software. The development process for mission-critical airplane software makes voting software look like a slapdash affair. If we care about the integrity of our elections, this has to change.

Proponents of DREs often point to successful elections as "proof" that the systems work. That completely misses the point. The fear is that errors in the software—either accidental or deliberately introduced—can undetectably alter the final tallies. An election without any detected problems is no more a proof that the system is reliable and secure than a night that no one broke into your house is proof that your locks work. Maybe no one tried to break in, or maybe someone tried and succeeded—and you don't know it.

Even if we get the technology right, we still won't be finished. If the goal of a voting system is to accurately translate voter intent into a final tally, the voting machine itself is only one part of the overall system. In the 2004 US election, problems with voter registration, untrained poll workers, ballot design, and procedures for handling problems, resulted in far more votes being left uncounted than problems with technology.

If we're going to spend money on new voting technology, it makes sense to spend it on technology that makes the problems easier instead of harder.

# Electronic Voting Is Better than Using Paper Ballots

*Michael Trice*

*Michael Trice was a student at the University of Texas at Austin when he wrote this viewpoint.*

I [once] worked for one of the four major providers of electronic voting machines in the United States. I left to go to graduate school and write the great American novel, not because of the industry.

Democracy needs to evolve with technology for the health of our nation and its founding principles. The freedom electronic voting allows for disabled voters, for certified and responsive voting and for accountability must not be dismissed because of our fear of change. All this means that House Bill 3894 represents the worst in reactionary political rabble-rousing.

## A Step Backward

As introduced by [Texas] representative Lon Burnam, HB 3894 attempts to undo the federal Help America Vote Act [HAVA] passed in 2002 to overcome all the issues that arose from the 2000 election. The 2006 election, with nationwide use of electronic voting machines, went along with nary an issue involving controversy arising from the security or vote-marking performance of the electronic voting machines used. In fact, for those who see all electronic voting machines as work of the great right-wing conspiracy, recent elections seem to dispel the force of the myth.

Yet the screams for retrograde action remain constant, so let us consider the cost of such action.

HAVA, when passed, came with federal funding to allow all counties the ability to replace their existing voting machines. Burnam's bill possesses no such funding. Maybe [Fort Worth's] Tarrant County has the ability to afford a switch in voting systems without missing a beat, but the last time I looked at some of Fort Worth's decaying infrastructure, I think there existed a few places those extra funds could be spent for improvements.

---

*Certainly electronic voting machines offered far less opportunity for traditional ballot confusion than paper ballots.*

---

Other counties may not possess Fort Worth's apparent excess of resources. Smaller, rural counties lack the funds to switch voting systems without suffering extreme consequences. Where these counties need improvements to roads, schools, healthcare and an aging population, HB 3894 demands more from limited resources. The money must come from somewhere—fear has a price.

## The Value of Electronic Voting

Two of the most significant driving forces behind electronic voting originated in the desire to create simple, unified ballots after the 2000 election and to increase independent access to anonymous voting for those with physical disabilities. The butterfly ballots of Miami-Dade and other areas created confusion and a desire for national elections to possess some ability for common audits.

Local counties and states maintained significant control even after HAVA, but certainly electronic voting machines offered far less opportunity for traditional ballot confusion than paper ballots. Ballot design still presented a handful of issues in 2006, pointing toward a need for uniform ballots more than an issue with the electronic voting machines displaying the ballots.

Additionally, electronic voting offers the best, most reliable method of voting for those with severe physical disabilities. Electronic voting machines make use of trackballs, breath tube interfaces and other features that allow independent voting in a thorough manner. Even Burnam recognizes this by providing the option of electronic marking devices for the physically disabled. Apparently, Burnam stops short of considering electronic voting unfit for all Americans.

We must question the validity of our fears. No one wants to claim electronic voting is foolproof, but paper ballots present more issues with "lost" votes and "stuffed" ballot boxes. Burnam's solution is to force every polling place to buy security cameras (even more money for those smaller counties to scratch up) and record the ballot boxes, because we all know how "foolproof" security cameras are by comparison to hacking into electronic machines with unpublished operating systems and classified source codes.

Colorado and California both use electronic voting machines which print a paper record that the voter confirms as they vote. This creates an obvious paper trail that the voter can track. Maybe Burnam should examine the common sense used in other states before imposing an undue burden on [Texas].

# The Predicted E-Voting Meltdown in the 2008 Elections Did Not Happen

*Todd R. Weiss*

*Todd R. Weiss is a reporter and blogger for* Computerworld, *a technology news and information magazine.*

Despite reports all day long about an assortment of e-voting machine problems in several U.S. states, no massive systemic meltdown occurred.

Despite widespread pre-election concerns about malfunctioning e-voting hardware, election officials, e-voting activists and experts said Election Day polling generally went well—even with the problems that did surface.

## Limited Problems

Pamela Smith, president of San Francisco-based e-voting watchdog group VerifiedVoting.org, said that constant reports of long lines at polls were predictable, given the attention focused on the race between Sen. Barack Obama (D-Ill.) and Sen. John McCain (R-Ariz.).

"We're hearing a variety of reports" about problems involving optical scanners or voters having difficulty voting a straight ticket. What's interesting, she said, is that voters were extra-vigilant while voting. When a scanner isn't working and an election official tells a voter that they will put the completed paper ballot into a special box where it will be counted later, "voters are calling to be sure that's correct," Smith said. "That is correct," but what's notable is that voters are checking in the first place.

"We've had a number of cases on some of the older systems in Philadelphia where a certain light didn't light up" to announce that the voter's votes were counted, leaving open whether the bulb was out or the votes weren't tabulated, Smith said. "It's hard to know, when there's no paper trail."

John Gideon, executive director of e-voting watchdog group, VotersUnite.org in Bremerton, Wash., said before polls closed that the problems he had heard about were pretty much what he expected. "I'm a bit surprised that there haven't yet been any big reports of failures," he said. "Of course, we still have tabulations coming up.

"We haven't had an election yet where the machines haven't failed somewhere."

---

*The election was like any other—with some troubles and difficulties as always.*

---

Mary Boyle, a spokeswoman for the Washington-based government watchdog group Common Cause, agreed that the election seemed to have gone smoothly, even with reports about voting delays and machine glitches.

"We know that problems that we predicted are occurring in more than several states," she said, pointing to long lines caused by insufficient numbers of machines, hardware breakdowns, inadequate supplies of paper ballots and other issues. Some of those problems are "leading to people leaving the polls without being able to vote," Boyle said.

At the same time, "we wouldn't characterize this as a meltdown" of the system. "In spite of [the problems], things are going along."

Even so, the problems that occurred, "reinforce [that] this is an election system that's not equipped to handle a high turnout," she said. "And the high turnout is fantastic. People are excited to vote and participate in their democracy, and that is a great thing. It seems like people are hanging in there and are determined to cast their votes."

Doug Lewis, the executive director of the Houston-based National Association of State Election Directors, a professional group that represents election officials in the U.S., said the election was like any other—with some troubles and difficulties as always. "None of it is ever perfect," Lewis said. "You go and have an election and no matter . . . how much you plan, some things just don't work on Election Day. But you're usually able to correct those problems quickly."

"The truth of the matter is [today's election problems] are not systemic, it's not overwhelming," Lewis said. "It's not going to cause an uproar. It's pretty much a normal Election Day, even though it's a heavy-turnout Election Day."

Election officials who investigated reports that came into election hotlines were often unable to duplicate or substantiate the reports, he said. "From our standpoint, we're not seeing enormous numbers of incidents reported that . . . you can tie down to actual problems," he said. "We see a whole lot of anecdotal problems that always get reported on Election Day, but when you ask for specifics, they tend to disappear."

## No Satisfactory System

In his organization's national update, Jon Greenbaum, the legal lead for e-voting watchdog group the Election Protection Coalition, said that problems reported with machine voting in Florida, California and other states show that the election community has not yet devised a satisfactory system. As far as solving the "machine problem" is concerned, "all we've done is gotten rid of punch cards and lever machines," he said.

"Some of that is due to problems within the machines themselves, and some is due to issues involving humans," he said. "This is an area that really calls out for some investment in terms of technology; greater uniformity would also help. If we had greater uniformity for the type of technology that is being used, it would be easier to fix problems. Take Virginia—you have eight or nine different types of equipment being used. You can't take voting machines from one jurisdiction and have another jurisdiction that needs them use them. You can't have the state stock up, because there are too many different types of machines used."

## Reports from Specific States

In Ohio, Jeff Ortega, a spokesman for Secretary of State Jennifer Brunner, said that with an expected voter turnout of 80%, there were some delays of up to an hour at some polling places. But most lines moved much faster than that across the state.

"The line issue has been a concern for Secretary Brunner for some time," he said.

In Ohio, there were "no major problems to speak of in terms of activities at the polls" across the state, he said. The problems that occurred included "some minor hiccups in various places around the state" related to the voter-verifiable paper printouts that are produced by touch-screen machines. In some cases, it took several tries to get the paper rolling as it's designed to, he said.

Leslie Amoros, press secretary for Pennsylvania Secretary of State Pedro A. Cortes, said that the elections went "really well." She acknowledged media reports of long lines and sporadic e-voting equipment problems in Philadelphia, Pittsburgh and other parts of the state, but she said such problems were resolved.

"That's typical Election Day fare," she said. "There have been a couple of voting systems going down, but they're being brought back up within five minutes. Overall, commonwealth-wide, things are going fairly well."

County election officials were directed to prepare for heavy turnouts—as high as 80%—which is very high, she said. "We have been working with counties for months to prepare for this."

There are 8.76 million registered voters in Pennsylvania for this election; that's an all-time record, she said. [In 2004], there were 8.37 million registered voters.

Jennifer Krell Davis, a spokeswoman for Florida Secretary of State Kurt S. Browning, said that there were only minor e-voting issues across the state, with the problems corrected as needed. "Those [problematic] machines have been replaced or repaired," Davis said several hours before polls closed. "Everything's going smoothly now, and we expect it to go as well for the rest of the day."

---

*What would make e-voting systems more trustworthy . . . are requirements for voter-verifiable paper trails.*

---

In Colorado, Rich Coolidge, a spokesman for the Secretary of State's office, said that no problems had been reported across the state by early afternoon. "Everything is going very smoothly," he said.

More than 1.7 million of the 2.6 million active registered voters in Colorado had voted by mail or early voting before Election Day, and total vote turnout was expected to exceed 90%.

G. Terry Madonna, a political pollster and director of the Center for Politics and Public Affairs at Franklin and Marshall College in Lancaster, Pa., has been watching elections for decades and said this one is apparently no more problematic than others in past years.

What would make e-voting systems more trustworthy, he said, are requirements for voter-verifiable paper trails so that accurate, secure records could be kept of each vote. "I've read the studies that came out after 2000 and 2004 . . . about all the difficulties, Madonna said. "My own belief is I'd rather have a paper trail . . . in any of the computer-assisted voting devices."

"We can do it for an [ATM]," he said. "Many states already have it. I'm a strong supporter of that."

Madonna said he's not worried about someone switching integrated chips and hacking machines, "I'm not a conspiracy guy," he said. "It's possible to remove a chip and replace it. I don't necessarily think that that's the problem. But I do think that with all the money we put into government problems, we put too little time and money into voting systems."

# No Type of Voting System Is Infallible

*Bob Sullivan*

*Bob Sullivan is a journalist who covers Internet scams and consumer fraud for MSNBC.*

The headline for voting technology 2008 might be this: Back where we started. Back to paper ballots, that is.

For the first time since touch-screen voting was invented, use of the high-tech voting machines has declined sharply. On Nov. 4, [2008,] the majority of Americans will be filling out their ballots using old-fashioned paper and No. 2 pencils.

But it's been a long, strange trip back to the beginning. The gyrations of America's voting rituals began with hanging chads [incompletely punched holes in paper ballots] in 2000. Then came the Help America Vote Act of 2002, which set aside $3 billion to upgrade America's antiquated ballot system. Then came the gold rush toward space-aged, touch-screen electronic voting systems. Next, computer scientists uncovered multiple security flaws in electronic vote machines, with the controversy culminating in an HBO film called "Hacking Democracy."

That was enough for election officials in California, Florida, Maryland, and several other states that have placed their pricey touch-screen machines in moth balls. Most have returned to a system that relies—at least in part—on pencils.

According to Election Data Services, nearly 10 million fewer ballots will be cast on electronic voting systems [in 2008] than in 2006. Then, 38 percent of the electorate was registered in districts that used touch-screen systems; today, only 33 percent do.

"When you think of the alternatives, you could go with flawed machines or just shift people off of them and encourage people to go back to old-fashioned methods," said security researcher Herbert Thompson of People Security, a critic of some electronic voting systems.

The retreat from technology, however, shouldn't be overstated. While 56 percent of Americans live in a district where voters will fill out paper ballots on Nov. 4, those ballots will be counted by optical-scan readers—a system that is a hybrid between paper and computers.

Optical scanning machines have won the day, at least in 2008. Since 2006, 86 districts have changed voting systems—all moving to optical readers. But Kimball Brace of Election Data Systems states that, despite the current trend, touch-screen systems have not fallen completely out of favor.

"This isn't a settled question.... It all depends on what happens," he said. "If we have a close election and/or have problems that highlight a certain type of machine, that could have significant impact on what we end up doing in the future."

Problems with touch-screen systems—known in the industry as DRE or direct-recording electronic machines—are well documented. A series of confrontations between computer security researchers and voting machine manufacturers left a grey cloud over their ability to ward off hackers. Private manufacturers like Diebold have repeatedly refused to turn over their proprietary software for inspection and audits by academics.

---

*No voting system is perfect.*

---

Meanwhile, charges of "vote-switching" at polling places continue. In West Virginia, a handful of early voters claimed this month that their votes had been switched from one candidate to another by touch-screen machines. Some voters caught the error, but others told local newspapers they believe their vote was cast for the wrong person.

Brace said that human error, rather than conspiracy, is likely to blame. Anyone with a touch-screen phone is familiar with the ritual of recalibration that follows a series of misclicks. Also, screens can register touches by hanging sleeves or other incidental contact. Finally, anyone who's ever used an ATM has likely discovered the difficulty of using the machine from an incorrect angle; it's easy to hit the wrong button if you are too tall or too short.

## Pencils Make Mistakes, Too

No voting system is perfect, Brace said. And those who worked hard to discredit touch-screen systems may end up lamenting the end result. Paper and pencil, for example, are hardly infallible.

---

*No matter what technology is used to cast ballots, change always introduces errors.*

---

"There are problems with optical scanners, most notably American voters," he said. "They seem to know how to foul up a ballot, particularly when the ballot is a piece of paper." Some might circle the candidates they prefer rather than fill in a box, for example, he said.

Thompson, the e-voting critic, also sees problems with paper. Each time a system becomes popular, he said, it faces greater likelihood of problems.

"These are what we call 'scale-oriented' problems in computer science," Thompson said. "This increased burden on paper increases the chance for a problem."

Complicating matters further for voters is the unprecedented change that's taken place inside the voting booth. No matter what technology is used to cast ballots, change always introduces errors, Brace said. More than 40 percent of voters will encounter a new voting tool this season, given that many voters only cast ballots during presidential election years.

"History shows us that the greatest likelihood of election errors occurs the first time a jurisdiction changes voting systems," Brace said. "While many of these jurisdictions have tested out their procedures in the past four years, it's the voters themselves—both newly registered and those that haven't voted since [the last election]—that could cause problems [in the next election]."

According to an Associated Press survey, 108 voting districts have switched from touch-screen to paper and optical ballots since the last election.

## The Benefits of Touch Screen

Brace laments the fall of touch-screen machines, because he says they can do some things better than any other voting technology. They are particularly adept at providing foreign-language ballots or accessible ballots for the blind, for example. And when programmed properly, they can make over-votes—when a voter accidentally picks two candidates for one office—impossible. And they provide quick vote tallies.

In larger districts using optical scan readers, the tally machines are generally available right at the polling place, allowing voters to leave with a "receipt" of their ballot and providing near-instant counting when polls close. But in smaller, rural districts, the ballots must be hand-carried to a central optical scanner, which delays the counting.

Barring some surprise event—such as a poor performance by optical scanners—Brace believes touch-screens will slowly disappear from voting booths around the country.

Counties that wanted Help America Vote Act money had to buy new systems by 2006. Many purchased touch-screen systems without fully examining them and are now warehousing the machines, Thompson said.

Without upgrades, there won't be a market for them, but touch-screen machines are unlikely to be fixed any time soon. The federal money that fueled their popularity is gone.

"These problems can be addressed but you need the investment money, and now the manufacturers have no incentive to fix them because there is no money," Thompson said.

# Electronic Voting Machines Invite Tampering

*Common Cause*

*Common Cause is a nonprofit, nonpartisan citizens' lobbying organization promoting open, honest, and accountable government.*

Serious questions about the reliability and security of paperless electronic voting machines known as Direct Recording Electronic (DRE) devices continue to be raised nationwide. Major security concerns have been documented . . . , and a number of states that held primary elections [in 2006] saw problems with DREs. Yet nearly 40 percent of voters are expected to cast ballots on DREs in November [2006], and Congress continues to ignore the problems. . . .

DREs are highly vulnerable to machine malfunction and human manipulation. The two largest concerns are their lack of transparency and the fact that they do not produce a backup system that can allow for a recount.

When a citizen casts a vote on an electronic voting machine, there is no way for that person to ensure that the vote was recorded correctly. Software code inside the machine can be programmed to display the correct vote on the voting screen, but the vote in fact could be recorded incorrectly. In other words, a citizen could pick candidate John Smith for president, and the screen could show that the citizen picked John Smith, but the computer could be programmed to record the vote for Bill Blue.

Because electronic voting machines do not produce an independently verifiable paper voting record, there is no good record that can be used for an audit or a recount. Although

"Malfunction and Malfeasance—A Report on the Electronic Voting Machine Debacle," Washington, DC: Common Cause, 2008. Reproduced by permission.

some electronic voting machines do keep paper records of the complete ballot image, not every machine does. And unfortunately, if the machine malfunctions or the computer code has been the subject of tampering, this record is no longer reliable.

---

*A number of studies and policy papers have concluded that DREs are vulnerable to tampering.*

---

In other words, there is no way to recount the vote tallies recorded by a DRE machine, nor is there any way to retrieve previously recorded votes if the data is erased or corrupted. Election officials must place their trust in the design and performance of the machine, despite the fact that the software is trade-secret protected and cannot be inspected, even by election officials in most cases. This lack of transparency and the lack of a back-up system makes these machines inappropriate for use in elections unless appropriate safeguards are put in place.

## Studies Show DREs Vulnerable

A number of studies and policy papers have concluded that DREs are vulnerable to tampering. . . .

In 2003, computer science professors from Johns Hopkins University, led by Dr. Avi Rubin, released one of the first widely circulated reports analyzing the security standards of a DRE system. In their report, "Analysis of an Electronic Voting System," which reviewed Diebold's AccuVote-TS systems, they found a string of vulnerabilities making the machines susceptible to tampering. For example, to operate the Diebold machines on Election Day, poll workers provide voters with "smartcards," which are required to be entered into the machine to record a vote. The study found that it would be relatively easy for somebody to program their own "smartcard" and manipulate data. They also found that someone could intercept machines' transfer information electronically and discovered weaknesses in the programming code. Dr. Rubin stated that he would have flunked a first-year student who turned in a program with such weak code. . . .

In 2005, the Government Accountability Office (GAO) released an extensive report assessing the significant security and reliability concerns that have been identified with electronic voting systems. The report, entitled "Federal efforts to improve security and reliability of electronic voting systems are under way, but key activities need to be completed," surveyed over 80 studies and research reports related to the security of electronic voting systems and focused on systems associated with vote casting and counting. The report noted that these studies listed a number of potential security flaws including weak security controls, system design flaws, inadequate system version control, inadequate security testing, incorrect system configuration, and poor security management. . . .

In their conclusion, the authors of the report noted that their review "pointed to a situation in which vendors may not be uniformly building security and reliability into their voting systems, and election officials may not always rigorously ensure the security and reliability of their systems when they acquire, test, operate and manage them."

---

*There are a number of instances where electronic voting machines have added or removed votes in real elections, throwing the outcome of the election into question.*

---

In 2005, the Commission on Federal Election Reform was established to research the state of elections in the United States and offer recommendations for improvement. The bipartisan commission was led by former Democratic President Jimmy Carter and former Republican Secretary of State James Baker. In September 2005, the commission released its broad set of reform proposals covering a wide array of election issues. Key among them were the issues presented by voting technology.

The commissioners surveyed existing reports, academic studies, and other material to formulate their recommendations for DRE technology. They concluded that the benefits of DREs were offset by a lack of transparency and noted that DREs do not allow voters to check [to see] if their ballot is recorded correctly and that some DREs have no capacity for an independent recount. In their final report, the commissioners recommended that Congress pass legislation requiring all voting systems to produce a voter verified paper record and that states adopt formal auditing procedures to reconcile any disparity between the electronic ballot tally and the paper ballot tally. . . .

In May 2006, Finnish computer security expert Harri Hursti, working with the organization BlackBoxVoting.org released a report documenting several security issues with the Diebold electronic voting terminals TSx and TS6. According to the report, "the security threats seem to enable a malicious person to compromise the equipment even years before actually using the exploit, possibly leaving the voting terminal incurably compromised." In other words, a computer hacker, doubling as a poll worker, would only need a few seconds of physical access to the machines to introduce a virus to the software by putting a memory card inside of the machine. Because the memory cards are transferred from one machine to another, this could cause the machines to fail or to simply change the vote outcome by switching votes.

## Actual Machine Failures

Problems with DREs are not theoretical. There are a number of instances where electronic voting machines have added or removed votes in real elections, throwing the outcome of the election into question. Below are just a few examples where voting machine failures were so egregious that they were detected.

During [the] Texas primaries in March [2006], a programming error caused voting machines in Tarrant County to record an additional 100,000 votes that were never actually cast. Election officials were shocked when the initial tallies showed that 158,000 voters came to the polls, a number that would have shattered the previous primary turnout record and more than doubled the turnout of 76,000 in 2002.

A programming mistake in the machine's software by a company responsible for both hardware and software, Hart Intercivic, boosted vote totals far beyond the 58,000 votes that were actually cast. The company said that the error boosted the totals equally for every candidate and that the election outcomes were not affected. . . .

In November 2004, 4,438 votes were lost by an electronic voting machine in Carteret County, North Carolina, leaving the race for state agricultural commissioner in limbo for months. On Election Night, 3.3 million ballots were cast and Republican Steve Troxler led Democrat Britt Cobb by 2,287 votes. With almost twice that amount of votes permanently erased, a contentious legal battle ensued that only ended three months later when Cobb decided to concede the election. . . .

In April 2005, Pennsylvania decertified the UniLect Patriot electronic voting machine after concluding that defects in the system were responsible for more than 10,000 uncounted votes in three different counties in November 2004. When the state re-examined the machines after the elections, it found that the machines often failed to register votes after the voter pressed the screen to make his or her selection. The machines were also prone to freezing up during use. . . .

During a special election on the issue of slot machines, Miami-Dade County's new Elections Systems & Software (ES&S) iVotronic electronic voting machines produced more than 1,200 undervotes, despite the fact that there was only one issue on the ballot. Undervotes are counted ballots that contain no votes for candidates or issues, and a high number of them typically indicates a problem with the machine. . . .

The elections supervisor, Lester Sola, has since recommended that the county replace their $25 million system for an optical scanning system, citing the decline in voter confidence and increasing costs associated with the current DRE system.

The failure of ten electronic voting machines [also] cast doubt on the results of a local election in Fairfax County, Virginia during November 2003. Voters claimed that the machines failed to register their votes for incumbent school board member Rita S. Thompson (R), who lost by 1,662 votes. When testing one of the questionable machines, elections officials observed that it appeared to subtract a vote from Thompson for about one out of every 100 attempts to vote for her. . . .

It was impossible to determine whether lost votes were intended for Thompson or whether other candidates also lost votes, and the questionable elections results were certified without any adjustment. . . .

---

*It is clear that we must take bold action to safeguard our elections, or it is likely that they will be compromised.*

---

## Bold Action Needed

Congress passed the Help America Vote Act (HAVA) in 2002 to rectify problems in our election system exposed during the 2000 presidential election. Plagued by the memory of election officials haggling over hanging chads, Congress included requirements calling for technological advances in election system machinery.

Many election officials perceived DREs as the best answer to some HAVA requirements. As a result, DRE use exploded.

The number of counties nationwide using DREs more than tripled [since 2000], jumping from 320 counties in November 2000 to an expected 1,050 counties in November's [2006] mid-term elections. About 39 percent of registered voters are expected to use DRE voting machines on Election Day 2006.

However, because these machines are proven to be prone to malfunction and failure and vulnerable to computer hacking, it is clear that we must take bold action to safeguard our elections, or it is likely that they will be compromised. Transparent methods for proving the accuracy of election tallies will help reassure voters that the election results are correct.

# Electronic Voting Puts Democracy in Peril

*David E. Scheim*

*David E. Scheim is an information systems consultant for a federal agency and author of the best-selling book* Contract on America.

In Maryland, a citizens' revolt against electronic voting machines has been launched by none other than the state's Republican governor. Gov. Robert Ehrlich advised Maryland residents to vote by absentee ballot because he had no confidence in the state's voting machines. Ehrlich explained to ABC News:

"I don't care if we paid half a billion dollars or $1 billion. If it's going to put the election at risk, there's no price tag for a phony election or a fraudulent election."

As *The New York Times* noted in a recent editorial, [the 2006] elections indeed "provided a lot of disturbing news about the reliability of electronic voting." And several prestigious studies have indeed recently sounded the alarm about turning over the election process, previously conducted transparently by local counties, to electronic voting machines subject to error and fraud controlled by corporations of questionable lineage.

A bipartisan Commission on Federal Election Reform, chaired by James A. Baker III and former President Jimmy Carter, warned in 2005 that election results could be electronically manipulated by malicious software modifications. The U.S. Government Accountability Office issued a damning report [in 2005] on electronic voting machines, citing widespread irregularities in recent elections.

The Brennan Center at New York University found 120 serious vulnerabilities in electronic voting machines and concluded that they "pose a real danger to the integrity of national, state and local elections." Verified voting, it determined, was necessary for reliable elections.

In September [2006], the Princeton University Center for Information Technology Policy demonstrated how software could be inserted into a Diebold electronic voting machine in less than a minute that switches votes from one candidate to another, without leaving any trace of the fraud.

The software, like a virus, can propagate from machine to machine. The Princeton video demonstration, has alarmed even former skeptics of these vulnerabilities.

## Changing Election Outcomes

By all indications, Diebold may have used exactly this technique to change the outcomes in key Georgia election races in 2002.

In October's [2006] *Rolling Stone*, Robert F. Kennedy Jr. detailed how national Diebold executive Bob Urosevich personally distributed a voting machine "patch" that was installed on some 5,000 Diebold voting machines in Georgia prior to that election.

According to Diebold insider Chris Hood, "It was an unauthorized patch" of questionable purpose, installed covertly at odd hours.

Other insider sources described other suspicious patches. In fact, significant leads in pre-election polls by the Democratic candidates for Senate and governor were reversed, respectively, by 8 and 12 points to switch expected victories into losses.

The same Bob Urosevich, the first CEO [chief executive officer] of Diebold, was also the founder of ES&S, another voting machine company.

These two companies tally 80 percent of U.S. votes, while former Diebold executives control the company that produces WINvote election machines, used in several Virginia counties.

Jeff Dean, a key programmer for Diebold, was convicted of 23 counts of felony theft for planting back doors in software he created for ATMs.

In a scathing 2004 editorial, *The New York Times* detailed the lax oversight, conflicts of interest, proprietary software and security risks characterizing electronic voting machines and their manufacturers, and contrasted this with the rigorous oversight and standards for electronic gambling machines in Nevada.

There is no federal agency to shut down Diebold, for example, for practices as described in this leaked e-mail of March 19, 1999: "For a demonstration [in Colorado] I suggest you fake it. . . . That is what we did in the last AT/AV [AccuTouch/AccuVote] demo."

Among several dozen cases of electronic voting machine irregularities nationwide were 6,300 electronic votes lost in the 2002 Alabama gubernatorial race, which flipped the election outcome.

In the 2006 primary election in Tarrant County, Texas, 100,000 more votes were recorded than actually cast, with some votes counted up to six times.

---

*Momentum to mandate verified voting is building at both the state and federal levels.*

---

In the [2006] election, in [controversial Florida secretary of state] Katherine Harris's former U.S. congressional district in Florida, Christine Jennings, the Democratic candidate, trails by 373 out of 237,861 votes because electronic voting machines lost 15,000 votes in a majority Democratic county. Hundreds of voters reported selecting Jennings without her name being registered.

Candidate names were truncated on the summary page by electronic voting machines in three Virginia counties, with the last name of one U.S. Senate candidate omitted.

And as documented by the Fairfax County Republican Committee, in a 2003 local election, at least one WINvote voting machine "subtracted one vote for every 100 cast in favor of a [Republican] candidate for the Fairfax School Board."

Momentum to mandate verified voting is building at both the state and federal levels.

# California Has Rejected Electronic Voting

*John Wildermuth*

*John Wildermuth is a reporter for the* San Francisco Chronicle *newspaper.*

Electronic voting systems used throughout California still aren't good enough to be trusted with the state's elections, [California] Secretary of State Debra Bowen said [on December 1, 2007].

While Bowen has been putting tough restrictions and new security requirements on the use of the touch screen machines, she admitted having doubts as to whether the electronic voting systems will ever meet the standards she believes are needed in California.

"It's a real challenge," she said at a San Francisco airport conference on voting and elections. "I don't rule out the ingenuity of some computer science student now in the eighth grade," but what's available now isn't as transparent or auditable as the paper ballot systems they replaced.

Earlier [in 2007], Bowen put together a top-to-bottom review of voting systems used in the state and found that most of the voting machines were vulnerable to hackers looking to change results or cause mischief with the systems.

Despite loud howls from county voting officials, Bowen decertified almost all the touch screen systems used in California, allowing only their most limited use.

"When the government finds a car is unsafe, it orders a recall," she said. "Here we're talking about systems used to cast and tally votes, the most basic tool of democracy."

In the Bay Area, Santa Clara and Napa counties found themselves forced to scramble to replace their electronic voting systems. San Mateo County uses the Hart eSlate system, a touch screen system Bowen said is relatively safe from hackers.

The secretary admitted that she wants to see California's counties use optical scan systems in their polling places, especially because most of them already use the systems to count mail ballots.

Optical scan systems, where voters mark their choices on a paper ballot that then gets inserted into a tallying machine, "are old and boring, but cheap and reliable," Bowen said, because the paper ballots make it easy to recount the ballots and ensure the accuracy of the vote.

"I want to make sure the votes are secure, auditable and transparent and that every vote is counted as it was cast," she said.

Although Bowen's review of the voting systems affected only California, it had a nationwide impact, because the same systems are used in many other states.

---

*Battles continue across the voting landscape, with election officials, voting machine manufacturers and . . . citizen activists all arguing over the direction the nation's voting rules should take.*

---

The review "was like a big rock tossed in a pond, which continues to ripple across the nation," said Doug Chapin of Electionline.org, the nonpartisan group that sponsored the conference.

## Continuing Debate

While Bowen hoped her decision on the voting machines would allow both election officials and voters "to stop worrying about how to cast our votes," that hasn't happened.

Battles continue across the voting landscape, with election officials, voting machine manufacturers and various citizen activists all arguing over the direction the nation's voting rules should take.

"The secretary of state has a strategic plan, and I disagree with it," Steven Weir, Contra Costa County's registrar, told the conference. "Her plan is to debase confidence in our voting system," and Bowen has excluded local election officials from decisions that affect them greatly.

Local election officials are under increasing scrutiny, much of it from people "looking to give themselves a partisan advantage, fair or not," Weir added.

"No election system is ever good enough for the candidate who loses the election," said John Lindback, director of the elections division for the Oregon secretary of state. Changes like the ranked choice voting system used in San Francisco are often pushed by people who "didn't like who won the last election or the last 10 elections" and are disguising them as election reform.

But many of the people most concerned about voting machines and election accuracy "are not conspiracy theory nutballs," said Pamela Smith of VerifiedVoting.org, which looks at voting problems across the nation. Some of the most passionate advocates for change are computer scientists concerned that election officials put too much trust in systems that experts know are all too fallible.

"It's critical to ratchet down the attack-defense mode" between election officials and voting activists to reach their joint goal of making elections work, she said.

At least one concern of the electronic voting opponents seems to be overblown, though. There has been no record of anyone hacking into a voting machine to change election results and only a handful of cases of any type of election fraud in the country, said Mike Slater of Project Vote, a nonpartisan voter registration group.

Between 2002 and 2005, only 24 people were convicted of voting fraud in the entire nation, and most of them mistakenly thought they were eligible [to vote, when they were not], he said.

"It's hard to study election fraud in America because there's not much of it," said Thad Hall, an assistant professor of political science at the University of Utah. "People make stupid mistakes, but fraud is a very different beast."

# Electronic Voting Machines Are Still Controversial

*Larry Greenemeier*

*Larry Greenemeier is a journalist who has written about busi-
ness and technology since 1996, primarily for* Scientific American *magazine.*

Electronic voting machines remain as iffy and controversial
as ever. The new technology was once widely viewed as an
improvement over the antiquated paper ballots used in some
states during the highly contentious 2000 presidential race
that ushered George W. Bush into the White House (think:
hanging chads). But it is still plagued by accuracy and security
concerns.

In a recent report, the Government Accountability Office
(GAO)—Congress's investigative arm—gave at best a luke-
warm endorsement of electronic voting technology. Congress
called upon the GAO to investigate the role that iVotronic
direct-recording electronic (DRE) touch-screen voting machines, made by Election Systems & Software, Inc., in Omaha,
Neb., played in the highly controversial 2006 election for
Florida's 13th Congressional District, in which Republican
Vern Buchanan edged out Democrat Christine Jennings by a
whisker-thin 369 vote margin.

During that election, more than 18,000 of the 143,532 ballots cast on the e-voting machines in Florida's Sarasota County
did not register a vote for either candidate. The GAO checked
for flaws in voting machines used there during the election. As
part of the effort, investigators examined the firmware
(software embedded in the devices) to make sure it matched
that certified by the State of Florida. They also tested the de-

vices to make sure they properly recorded and counted the ballots and whether they could provide accurate results even if miscalibrated.

The agency's conclusion: "Although the test results cannot be used to provide absolute assurance, we believe that these test results, combined with the other reviews that have been conducted by Florida, GAO, and others, have significantly reduced the possibility that the iVotronic DREs were the cause of the undervote."

Although hardly a ringing endorsement for e-voting technology, the GAO's findings contradicted those of researchers at Dartmouth College and the University of California, Los Angeles, who, after conducting a separate study found that the "exceptionally high . . . undervote rate" in the Florida 13th District race "was almost certainly caused by" a poorly designed and confusing electronic ballot displayed on the voting machine's touch screen.

Florida's own assessment of its e-voting technology statewide has been even less enthusiastic. The state commissioned a review led by Florida State University's Security and Assurance in Information Technology (SAIT) laboratory of voting system software made by Diebold Election Systems (which now calls itself Premier Election Solutions). Two months later, investigators released a scathing report in which they describe a glitch in Diebold's optical-scan firmware that enabled a "type of vote manipulation if an adversary can introduce an unofficial memory card into an active terminal" prior to an election. Such a card can be preprogrammed to essentially swap the electronically tabulated votes of two candidates or reroute all of one candidate's votes to a different candidate. The investigators simulated a cyber strike on their test systems and had no trouble carrying it out despite new mechanisms designed to protect against "similarly documented attacks in previous studies," the report states.

SAIT also found that the systems' encryption algorithms "had some cryptographic flaws," says SAIT co-director Alec Yasinsac, a Florida State University associate professor of computer science. In particular, the keys required to lock and unlock encrypted information were difficult to manage and safeguard against potential hackers. Once they cracked the encryption code, investigators found, intruders were able to access all encrypted data in the voting machine. "These types of attacks are very real," he says.

One of the greatest challenges when securing computers is accounting for the unexpected, says Seth Hallem, CEO of Coverity, Inc., the San Francisco-based maker of the source code analysis software that SAIT used during its probe of Diebold's system. This is becoming more difficult as increasingly sophisticated software—including that which runs electronic voting machines—continues to grow to encyclopedic portions. One program can contain tens of millions of lines of code.

Whereas certain technology—such as pacemakers and other medical devices—are heavily regulated and must adhere to strict design and construction standards, voting machines are still mostly unregulated. "There's no validation of how the software for these systems is designed and built," Hallem says, adding that this is "surprising given the importance of voting machines to our national infrastructure."

This has caused problems throughout the U.S. as different states attempt to assess the effectiveness of their e-voting technology. Following a review of e-voting machine security vulnerabilities and source code, California Secretary of State Debra Bowen in August decertified all e-voting machines in her state, other than those designed for disabled voters. Ohio Secretary of State Jennifer Brunner recently released the results of a probe into her state's electronic voting systems that concluded they, too, were riddled with "critical security failures" that could impact the integrity of elections.

"In the year 2000, when the Florida election went nuts, there were some electronic systems, but by and large the vast majority was done on handwritten ballots and punch ballots," SAIT co-director Yasinsac says. In the wake of the controversy, e-voting was held up as a way to restore integrity to the process. "We pushed this technology even though it was not ready," he adds. "Much of the software that the machines used is more than 10 years old and has been revised heavily, making it harder to review."

# CHAPTER 3

# Is the U.S. Elections System Fair?

# Chapter Preface

One aspect of fairness in the federal elections system concerns the financial burden of running a campaign for federal office. In recent years, these costs have reached astronomical levels, and they rise ever higher each election cycle. Today, only incumbents and prospective candidates who can amass huge amounts of money have any hope of winning federal-level public office; those without connections to big money sources simply have no chance. Because of these concerns, campaign finance reform has been a major issue in America for many decades.

Since 1907, U.S. law has barred corporations from contributing funds to candidates for federal office, and later laws required candidates and parties to disclose information about campaign contributors. The first modern campaign finance reform was the Federal Election Campaign Act (FECA), a 1971 law that strengthened earlier disclosure requirements for candidates and parties and extended these requirements to political parties and political action committees (PACs), groups formed to raise money for political candidates. In addition, FECA limited the amount federal candidates could contribute to their own campaigns as well as the amounts that could be spent on all media advertising, including television, radio, magazines, newspapers, and billboards.

Other reforms followed in the wake of Watergate, the political scandal that led to the resignation of then-president Richard Nixon in 1974. The most significant reform of this period was an amendment to FECA that virtually rewrote the original law. An important part of the new FECA was a program of public campaign funding for presidential elections. This program allows U.S. presidential candidates to opt for full public financing for presidential general election campaigns and partial subsidies for presidential primary campaigns in exchange for limiting private donations. Its purpose is to reduce the pressures of raising money for campaigns and encourage candidates to solicit small donations. The program operates through a voluntary contribution on federal income tax forms.

The 1974 FECA law also strengthened disclosure provisions and set new limits on campaign contributions and expenditures. Individual contribution limits were set at $1,000 per candidate, an additional $1,000 for candidate advertising, $5,000 for donations to PACs, and an aggregate amount of $25,000 for all contributions to all federal candidates, parties, or PACs. PACs were permitted to collect only small donations of $5,000 each year from individuals, and were limited to spending $5,000 per candidate. Candidates themselves were limited to spending only $50,000 of their own money if they wanted to accept public financing. To enforce these provisions, the act created an independent agency—the Federal Election Commission (FEC).

A 1976 U.S. Supreme Court decision in *Buckley v. Valeo*, however, seriously undermined FECA by ruling that the act of spending money for political campaigns is entitled to constitutionally guaranteed free speech protections. The Court's ruling struck down all of FECA's spending limits as well as limits on contributions made by candidates themselves or made by citizens or PACs for so-called independent expenditures, such as advertising that was not directly connected with a candidate's campaign. By allowing unlimited amounts to be spent on campaigns and approving independent expenditures, the *Buckley* decision unleashed a new wave of corporate money into elections, much of it spent on "issue ads"—expensive television advertisements usually funded by PACs set up by corporations and other special interest groups.

Additional loopholes were also found to circumvent campaign spending constraints. Using one technique called "bundling," for example, individuals (or companies) can collect large numbers of individual contributions from family members, friends, or employees and then deliver the combined donation to a particular candidate. Another loophole is known as "soft money," which refers to funds not regulated by federal laws. Because state and local political parties complained that the FECA spending limits restricted them from doing grassroots political activities such as voter registration and get-out-the-vote drives, Congress passed new amendments to FECA in 1979 granting party organizations the right to collect and spend unlimited amounts of money on these activities. Soon, however, political parties began funding issue ads as well, stretching the limits of FECA to new levels and allowing parties to become the primary sponsor of expensive issue ads.

The most recent reform was the 2002 Bipartisan Campaign Reform Act (BCRA), often called McCain-Feingold after its Senate sponsors, John McCain and Russ Feingold. BCRA closed the soft money loophole and increased the limits for direct individual contributions to campaigns, allowing individuals to contribute $2,000 in primary elections and $2,000 in general elections for each individual candidate, up to certain limits. BCRA also provided that ads that refer to a federal candidate cannot be broadcast within thirty days of a primary and sixty days of an election. Wealthy donors and candidates, however, quickly figured out how to get around BCRA's soft money ban—through the use of tax-exempt political organizations known as "527"s, named after a provision of the U.S. tax code. These 527 groups function like PACs, but are not regulated by the FEC and can collect and spend unlimited amounts on issue ads. As a result, 527 groups have proliferated, and so far, no legislation has been passed to regulate them.

Today, because of these weaknesses in U.S. campaign finance laws, it costs more than ever to campaign for national office. Experts say that competitive U.S. Senate races average about $34 million per campaign. Presidential elections, too, cost more each year. According to the *Wall Street Journal*, the 2008 presidential race cost a total of about $1.6 billion, double the cost of the presidential race in 2004.

Although finding a perfect solution to the problem of campaign finance may not be possible, the most popular ideas appear to be public funding and free (or cheap) TV airtime. In fact, a grassroots movement has been gaining ground in America to push for a public funding approach in state elections. This approach, called Clean Money/Clean Elections, was embraced by Maine in 1996 and has since been enacted by sixteen states. Similar federal-level legislation—called Fair Elections Now—was introduced in 2009 in the U.S. Senate by Dick Durbin and Arlen Specter and in the U.S. House of Representatives by John Larsen and Walter Jones. Although this federal legislation has not yet passed, it would provide public funding for candidates running for Congress. Advocates of public funding claim that it encourages a wider array of qualified candidates to run for office and allows candidates to spend less time raising money and more time discussing issues and interacting with voters—changes that lead to more substantive, issue-oriented elections and less apathy among voters.

Campaign finance reform, however, is only one effort to improve federal elections. The commentators in the viewpoints in this chapter debate other issues that may affect the fairness of federal elections, including the electoral college system, the role of race in national politics, and the impact of voter suppression efforts.

# The Electoral College System Is a Brilliant Constitutional Device

*Tara Ross*

*Tara Ross is a lawyer and writer and the author of* Enlightened Democracy: The Case for the Electoral College.

The election of 2000 caused many Americans to focus, perhaps for the first time, on the existence of the Electoral College. Few voters seemed to have strong feelings about the system one way or another prior to the election. *After* the election, many voters quickly developed passionate opinions regarding the wisdom of awarding the presidency based upon states' votes rather than individuals' votes. Some Americans seem to have become instant Electoral College opponents or supporters, depending on which candidate they backed in the voting booth that year.

How unfortunate. The Electoral College is a brilliant constitutional device that deserves the support of the American people. It does not deserve such support, however, simply because one man in one year won one election—nor does it deserve to be opposed because one man lost one election. It should be evaluated and judged on its own merits, regardless of which candidate a person voted for in 2000. A fair evaluation of the system reveals that it is the perfect complement to the other checks and balances in the Constitution.

We hear much talk today about efforts to "spread democracy" in the Middle East and elsewhere. Americans quickly and easily speak of our own country as a democracy. But the founding generation would not have been so quick to use the same description. To the contrary, patriots such as James

Tara Ross, "The Electoral College," *The Federalist Society Online Debate Series*, October 28, 2008. Reproduced by permission.

Madison, Benjamin Rush, and Fisher Ames described democracies as "spectacles of turbulence and contention," "the greatest of evils," and a "volcano, which conceals the fiery materials of its own destruction." The delegates to the convention never sought to create a pure democracy. They knew that such a government, in its purest form, could allow even "inflamed" majorities and "unreflective mob[s]" to rule. Freedom and self-government can co-exist only if devices are created to temper the momentary passions of the public. Thus, the Constitution they drafted includes several protections for minority interests and small states: a Senate in which each state has equal representation, a presidential veto, and supermajority requirements for certain types of governmental action. The Electoral College is a protective device that operates in this same spirit.

Some will argue at this juncture that the Electoral College is a protective device that was once needed, but that it has become outdated. Not so. Of course, some things have changed: The communication problems of the 18th century have been replaced by 24-hour news networks, Blackberrys, and the Internet. Many economic and commercial concerns are more international and less local than they once were. But the more fundamental aspects of our world have not changed. Power still corrupts. Self-government still suffers when ambition, greed, and individual selfishness run rampant. Minorities still need to be protected. Some states are still smaller than others, and each state has unique interests that should be represented in the federal government. Moderation and compromise among voters, political parties, and presidential candidates are still beneficial. Americans still need a President who represents the variety of subcultures that span the nation, rather than a President who only represents isolated regions, urban areas, or special interest groups. Finally, voters still need tools to help protect them against fraud and mistakes in the election process. The Electoral College continues to provide all these benefits to our country.

Discontent with the Electoral College is a real factor in America. But the cure is not elimination of the system. The Electoral College tends to be unsupported because it is not understood. To the degree that voter dissatisfaction exists, the appropriate solution is education about the history of and justifications for the system. This education will reveal that the Electoral College serves a critical role in our republican democracy.

# The Election of Barack Obama Has Restored the Faith of Blacks in America's Fairness

*Ward Connerly*

*Ward Connerly is a conservative Republican and the author of a memoir,* Lessons from My Uncle James: Beyond Skin Color to the Content of Our Character.

A s I watched tears flow down the cheeks of the Rev. Jesse Jackson during the speech of President-elect Barack Obama on election night, I fully understood the source of those tears. Not only was this one of those magical moments in the history of our nation, the occasion of a self-identified black man becoming the 44th president of the United States was an event of unparalleled joy and reflection for all of those, such as Jackson, who have lived with the humiliation of having their skin color used against them in American life.

Watching Jackson caused me to realize that the election of Obama was less about Obama than it was about Jackson, other blacks and our beloved country. For me, I thought of my Uncle James, a man who never got beyond the third grade, primarily because of his skin color; who was always consigned to the most menial and back-breaking jobs in our society, because of his skin color; who was called a "boy" by many Southern whites well into his third decade because of his skin color; and who was denied access to certain restaurants and public accommodations because of his skin color.

I thought of the psychological damage that had been done to generations of people who had just "one drop" of black blood, because of their skin color; the constant message that "you're not good enough, you're inferior" because of skin color. I thought of the fact that when he was born, Obama's parents could not marry in many states of our nation, because of skin color.

It has not escaped me that on the day that America elected its first black president—a true milestone for champions of civil rights—the people of arguably one of the most liberal states in the country were proclaiming that the right of gays to "marry" needed to be stripped from the California Constitution. Moreover, I note that black people, who have fought valiantly throughout their history for human dignity and their civil rights, cast their votes in substantial numbers against the marriage right of same-sex couples, even taking offense that the right to marry is compared to "civil rights."

The unfortunate aspect of racial "firsts" is the tendency to overstate the symbolism and to understate the substance. Somewhat lost in the historic hoopla of Obama's victory is the fact that his election represents a potentially profound changing of the guard about the direction of our country. I will leave it to others to decide whether some of the changes that he is likely to propose will be good or bad, but the direction proposed by Obama will undoubtedly be decidedly different from that of Sen. John McCain regarding a host of issues.

---

*There are so many problems in our country that go unattended because we approach them from a race-attentive perspective when, in fact, the problems transcend race.*

---

In the interest of full disclosure, I voted for McCain; and I have no regrets for having done so. President-elect Obama ran a brilliant campaign and he impressed me with his poise, temperament and extraordinary communication skills, but I found myself unalterably troubled by my perception that Sen. Obama would support a level of government that would be too intrusive for my taste. Given my ideological disagreement on this score, it would have been the height of hypocrisy for me to vote for Obama.

That would have been a triumph of color over principle.

All Americans, whether we voted for him or not, now own stock in the presidency of Barack Obama. He now belongs to all of us, not just to blacks or "progressives," but all of us. He deserves a chance to succeed, although we have a tendency to be unkind rather hastily to our sitting presidents. George W. Bush, for example, is no dummy, as many often characterize him. He is a very decent man for whom fate dealt a very bad hand that was worsened, perhaps, by a lot of human error. Someday, something similar will likely have to be said of President Obama.

It would be naïve and wrong-headed to suggest that all racism, from whatever source, has ended because of the symbolism of this one election. Yet what a symbol it is upon which we can have a new racial beginning, a beginning that accepts the dignity of every individual! For my fellow blacks, this is a time not just to celebrate, but to reflect upon where we go from here.

Throughout our history, we have allowed ourselves to be depicted as helpless and subject to the mercy of what others would do for us. "Affirmative action" is a classic example of that way of thinking. I consider that self-defeating and a betrayal of the enormous contributions that we have made to our country and to the considerable talents that reside within us. Liberation from this debilitating paradigm is now possible. Indeed, it is essential.

There are so many problems in our country that go unattended because we approach them from a race-attentive perspective when, in fact, the problems transcend race. By listening to some, one would think that the criminal justice system simply swallows up young black males. In fact, the system is inherently flawed and ill-serves all of us. Young white women can also be found in abundance in our federal correctional institutions serving long sentences for first-time white-collar offenses when they could be home wearing ankle bracelets and working to make restitution for their crimes.

On the night of Nov. 4, my faith in the fairness of the American people was validated. It is time now to move past the racial implications of the 2008 election and to confront the problems that afflict our human family in a nonracial fashion. All of us should regard this election as more than a good faith deposit on America's ability to be fair; it should be seen as an escrow closer. We should liberate ourselves from the past and all of the racial baggage that had been heaped on our shoulders. I am hopeful that President-elect Obama will make this one of his primary objectives.

# Allegations of Voter Fraud Are Greatly Exaggerated

*Justin Levitt*

*Justin Levitt is a lawyer at the Brennan Center for Justice, a nonpartisan public policy and law institute at New York University School of Law that focuses on fundamental issues of democracy and justice.*

Allegations of election-related fraud make for enticing press. Many Americans remember vivid stories of voting improprieties in Chicagoland, or the suspiciously sudden appearance of LBJ's [former president Lyndon B. Johnson's] alphabetized ballot box in Texas, or Governor Earl Long's quip: "When I die, I want to be buried in Louisiana, so I can stay active in politics." Voter fraud, in particular, has the feel of a bank heist caper: roundly condemned but technically fascinating, and sufficiently lurid to grab and hold headlines.

Perhaps because these stories are dramatic, voter fraud makes a popular scapegoat. In the aftermath of a close election, losing candidates are often quick to blame voter fraud for the results. Legislators cite voter fraud as justification for various new restrictions on the exercise of the franchise. And pundits trot out the same few anecdotes time and again as proof that a wave of fraud is imminent.

Allegations of widespread voter fraud, however, often prove greatly exaggerated. It is easy to grab headlines with a lurid claim ("Tens of thousands may be voting illegally!"); the follow-up—when any exists—is not usually deemed newsworthy. Yet on closer examination, many of the claims of voter fraud amount to a great deal of smoke without much fire. The allegations simply do not pan out.

These inflated claims are not harmless. Crying "wolf" when the allegations are unsubstantiated distracts attention from real problems that need real solutions. If we can move beyond the fixation on voter fraud, we will be able to focus on the real changes our elections need, from universal registration all the way down to sufficient parking at the poll site.

Moreover, these claims of voter fraud are frequently used to justify policies that do not solve the alleged wrongs, but that could well disenfranchise legitimate voters. Overly restrictive identification requirements for voters at the polls—which address a sort of voter fraud more rare than death by lightning—is only the most prominent example. . . .

## What Is Voter Fraud?

"Voter fraud" is fraud by voters.

More precisely, "voter fraud" occurs when individuals cast ballots despite knowing that they are ineligible to vote, in an attempt to defraud the election system.

*When every problem with an election is attributed to "voter fraud," it appears that fraud by voters is much more common than is actually the case.*

This sounds straightforward. And yet, voter fraud is often conflated, intentionally or unintentionally, with other forms of election misconduct or irregularities.

There are many such problems that are improperly lumped under the umbrella of "voter fraud." Some result from technological glitches, whether sinister or benign: for example, voting machines may record inaccurate tallies due to fraud, user error, or technical malfunction. Some result from honest mistakes by election officials or voters: for example, a person with a conviction may honestly believe herself eligible to vote when the conviction renders her temporarily ineligible, or an election official may believe that certain identification documents are required to vote when no such requirement exists. And some irregularities involve fraud or intentional misconduct perpetrated by actors other than individual voters: for example, flyers may spread misinformation about the proper locations or procedures for voting; thugs may be dispatched to intimidate voters at the polls; missing ballot boxes may mysteriously reappear. These are all problems with the election administration system . . . but they are not "voter fraud."

Conflating these concerns is not merely a semantic issue. First, the rhetorical sloppiness fosters the misperception that fraud by voters is prevalent. That is, when every problem with an election is attributed to "voter fraud," it appears that fraud by voters is much more common than is actually the case.

This, in turn, promotes inappropriate policy. By inflating the perceived prevalence of fraud by voters, policymakers find it easier to justify restrictions on those voters that are not warranted by the real facts.

Moreover, mislabeling problems as "voter fraud" distracts attention from the real election issues that need to be resolved. It draws attention away from problems best addressed, for example, by resource allocation or poll worker education or implementation of longstanding statutory mandates, and instead improperly focuses on the voter as the source of the problem. . . .

## Voter Fraud and Photo IDs

The most common example of the harm wrought by imprecise and inflated claims of "voter fraud" is the call for in-person photo identification requirements. Such photo ID laws are effective *only* in preventing individuals from impersonating other voters at the polls—an occurrence more rare than getting struck by lightning.

By throwing all sorts of election anomalies under the "voter fraud" umbrella, however, advocates for such laws artificially inflate the apparent need for these restrictions and undermine the urgency of other reforms.

Moreover, as with all restrictions on voters, photo identification requirements have a predictable detrimental impact on eligible citizens. Such laws are only potentially worthwhile if they clearly prevent more problems than they create. If policymakers distinguished real voter fraud from the more common election irregularities erroneously labeled as voter fraud, it would become apparent that the limited benefits of laws like photo ID requirements are simply not worth the cost.

---

*Often, what appears to be voter fraud—a person attempting to vote under a false name, for example—can be traced back to a typo.*

---

Royal Masset, the former political director for the Republican Party of Texas, concisely tied all of these strands together in a 2007 *Houston Chronicle* article concerning a highly controversial battle over photo identification legislation in Texas. Masset connected the inflated furor over voter fraud to photo identification laws and their expected impact on legitimate voters:

Among Republicans it is an "article of religious faith that voter fraud is causing us to lose elections," Masset said. He doesn't agree with that, but does believe that requiring photo IDs could cause enough of a dropoff in legitimate Democratic voting to add 3 percent to the Republican vote.

This remarkably candid observation underscores why it is so critical to get the facts straight on voter fraud. The voter fraud phantom drives policy that disenfranchises actual *legitimate* voters, without a corresponding actual benefit. Virtuous public policy should stand on more reliable supports.

## The Truth About Voter Fraud

There have been a handful of substantiated cases of individual ineligible voters attempting to defraud the election system. But by any measure, voter fraud is extraordinarily rare.

In part, this is because fraud by individual voters is a singularly foolish and ineffective way to attempt to win an election. Each act of voter fraud in connection with a federal election risks five years in prison and a $10,000 fine, in addition to any state penalties. In return, it yields at most one incremental vote. That single extra vote is simply not worth the price.

## Benign Errors Mistaken for Fraud

Instead, much evidence that purports to reveal voter fraud can be traced to causes far more logical than fraud by voters. [There are many] . . . common ways in which more benign errors or inconsistencies may be mistaken for voter fraud.

In the course of millions of recorded votes and voters, it is virtually certain that there will be clerical errors. Often, what appears to be voter fraud—a person attempting to vote under a false name, for example—can be traced back to a typo. . . .

The most common source of superficial claims of voter fraud, and the most common source of error, probably involves matching voter rolls against each other or against some other source to find alleged double voters, dead voters, or otherwise ineligible voters. . . .

Those searching for fraud—politicians, pundits, and even occasionally prosecutors—sometimes jump to unwarranted conclusions with a limited amount of information. The "birthdate problem" . . .—mistaking two different people with the same name and birthdate—is one example. But there are many other circumstances in which observers draw illicit conclusions from data that in fact have a benign explanation. . . .

Voter "caging" [, as another example,] is a tactic involving a mass mailing to registered voters to sniff out mailings that are returned undelivered; these undelivered mailings are then used to compile a list of voters allegedly enrolled under invalid addresses. But for many reasons, undelivered mail need not be an indication that a person registered at the given address is not entitled to vote there. A voter may be away from home for work, like a Louisiana Congresswoman challenged because she received her mail in Washington; or for military service, like an Ohio servicewoman challenged because she received her mail where she was stationed, in North Carolina; or for an extended vacation, like an Oregon woman rendered inactive because she was out of the country for a few months. A voter may live with others but be unlisted on the mailbox. Or, like Ohio resident Raven Shaffer, he may receive mail at a post office box or other mail service, and not at his registered residence. Moreover, some mail is simply not delivered, through no fault of the voter: in the 1990 census, for example, *The New York Times* reported that "[a]lthough at least 4.8 million [census] forms were found to be undeliverable by the Postal Service, 1.8 million of those were later delivered by hand." And recent reports found that government records used by Chicago postal workers to deliver mail contained more than 84,000 errors.

---

*Of the relatively small number of ineligible voters who mistakenly cast ballots, most are citizens rendered ineligible by criminal conviction.*

---

Mail sent to a listed registration address may also be returned as undeliverable because the voter has moved—even though the citizen remains wholly eligible to vote without reregistration. Each state has different rules determining when a voter who has moved must inform election officials of her new address. At a minimum, however, federal law provides that if a voter has moved within the same area covered by a given polling place—if, for example, a voter moves from one apartment to another within the same apartment complex, as a 2000 Oregon voter did—she may legitimately vote at that polling place even if she has not yet notified a registrar of her move. Similarly, a voter who has moved within the same registrar's jurisdiction and Congressional district may return to vote at her former polling place without re-registering. Especially in urban areas where there is high mobility within a particular neighborhood, undeliverable mail may simply reflect the recent move of a voter who remains fully eligible to vote. . . .

## Voter Mistakes

Even after accounting for the false conclusions above, investigations reveal that ineligible voters do sometimes cast votes. It is important, however, to distinguish those cases in which voters know they are ineligible but vote anyway—real voter fraud—from cases in which ineligible voters mistakenly believe themselves to be eligible. Both scenarios are unquestionably of concern. But it is likely to be more productive to address mistakes with remedies different from those often proposed for fraud.

Of the relatively small number of ineligible voters who mistakenly cast ballots, most are citizens rendered ineligible by criminal conviction. The laws concerning eligibility vary from state to state and can be confusing: different voters are disenfranchised for different convictions for different lengths of time. Moreover, the process of restoring a citizen's right to vote varies as well, from automatic restoration upon release from prison in states like Pennsylvania, Indiana, Ohio, Illinois, and Michigan, to the excruciatingly burdensome application process in Kentucky—which requires all would-be voters to submit a written application accompanied by three character references, an essay explaining why they should be eligible to vote, and a filing fee.

These rules are not merely difficult for voters to navigate: election officials with special training in the rules and regulations governing eligibility routinely get the law wrong. A 2004 survey, for example, found that 43% of New Jersey's county election offices did not follow state law in restoring citizens' right to vote. In New York, a much-publicized 2003 survey found that more than half of the local election officials did not follow state law; when the survey was repeated just two years later, 38% of the local boards of elections still got the law wrong.

It is difficult to expect disenfranchised voters to navigate the election laws successfully when so many election officials with expertise do not. Indeed, in Milwaukee, one voter asked to present identification at the polls showed his Department of Corrections ID card, with "OFFENDER" printed in bold letters across the face—but he was not informed by any poll worker that he might be ineligible to cast a ballot. Such cases show confusion . . . but not voter fraud.

# The Electoral College Should Be Eliminated

*Roy T. Davis*

*Roy T. Davis is a retired businessman and a lifelong Republican.*

Over my many years of voting, I have given the Electoral College only a passing moment of thought, as I think most Americans do. I was under the mistaken belief that it was just a formality, a part of our election process that changed nothing and affected nothing. I thought my vote in New York was cast for a Presidential and Vice Presidential candidate and that was that.

Then came the election of 2000 which drove home to me the shortcomings of the Electoral College. In that election it worked in favor of George Bush, who won when he actually had almost 500,000 fewer votes than Al Gore. I remember thinking at the time this was a peculiar outcome for our democracy. A man wins the most votes but he loses the election. What's wrong with this picture? The Electoral College, that's what and we shouldn't just shrug our shoulders and ignore this deficiency any longer. . . .

## Problems with the Electoral College

It's a good time to think about this antiquated process that the Electoral College forces upon us. Events in our country and the world are far too important today to allow it to determine elections. Not to mention it is grossly unfair for those who cast their ballots for the losing candidate in New York and consequently their vote does not count in the national total.

We now have intelligent (?), well funded and unscrupulous politicians and their party apparatuses who manipulate the

Roy T. Davis, "Electoral College Revisited," *EmpirePage.com*, October 28, 2008. Reproduced by permission of the author.

system. They are self serving with only one thing in mind and that is for them to stay in power. To them, their sole purpose is not to tackle and solve difficult, complex problems that we elected them to deal with but just to stay in power. Today they can do that very easily with the Electoral College by winning only eleven states!

It appears there are many and varied reasons why the Electoral College exists depending on who you read or listen to. The fact is it was developed 200 years ago and has a structure to it that was meant to appease opposing forces back then so they could agree on other issues. With that being said, it doesn't really matter how or why it's in place, it just is and we should seriously consider eliminating it and go to a straight popular vote election.

Consider this: any vote cast for a Presidential and Vice Presidential candidate who does not carry a state, other than Maine or Nebraska, counts for nothing toward the national accumulation of popular votes for those candidates. The ballots cast mean nothing. The only thing that matters are which candidate won each state by popular vote and those winning votes are the only ones that count. The process is a winner take all for Electoral College delegates by state. So, if my candidate didn't win the most votes in New York, my vote counts for nothing on the national total. Now here is the clincher: we never vote for a Presidential candidate anyway! That's right, we vote for a state Electoral College delegate in a political party who then is pledged to vote for whoever won the most votes in our state. Losing votes are thrown out.

The number of electoral delegates for each state is determined by the state population exactly the same as how the House of Representatives are chosen, plus two more delegates for each senator and two for Washington DC. The delegates are selected by political parties so if their candidate wins the popular vote IN EACH STATE; those delegates are pledged to vote the candidate of their party who won the state.

This is where I have a problem with the Electoral College. I am voting in a national election for President and Vice President not in a state election as the system is set up for now. Even when my candidate loses in New York, my vote should be counted in his or her national total of accumulated votes. That's why I'm voting, not for a state delegate to vote.

---

*Slick politicians can focus their money and energy on a very narrow number of states in order to win.*

---

## The New York Example

New York State is a good example of the deficiencies in the current system. Most heavily populated areas in our country like New York City have a large powerful Democratic Party organization which gives them a solid majority over other parties in the state each election cycle. That in itself is no cause to whine about them winning elections. They work hard to keep their power intact, obviously much harder than the Republicans, etc. In state elections, the candidate with the most votes wins. That's how we elect our Governor, etc. It's democracy; it's simple, it works and it's fair. Not so the Electoral College. . . .

Maine and Nebraska elect their Electoral College delegates exactly the same way they vote for their House of Representative candidates. It's not a winner take all but rather the way a democracy should work, by popular vote. The candidates running for President and Vice President in those two states get the number of delegates they deserve based on the popular vote received. It's so simple and the proper way for a democracy to function yet politicians and the media seem to find no fault with the Electoral College. I am more than a little distressed that my losing vote counts for nothing on the national total.

The real crux of the problem is that every vote cast in New York State, or any other state for that matter except the two mentioned above, for a losing Presidential candidate does not count. But suppose that candidate carries a state by a large margin of popular votes which, combined with the losing votes in New York would put him ahead in the total carried. It doesn't matter because of the Electoral College. This has brought us to modern times where these slick politicians can focus their money and energy on a very narrow number of states in order to win. It leads to manipulating elections that our politicians are getting very good at.

How much time in the last several national elections have candidates spent in New York State? Hardly any at all and particularly when you look at what they spend in the so called battleground states. New York has a guaranteed 31 electoral votes to the Democratic Party column. At the very least, if the popular votes were counted, both parties would win something and have to make some sort of effort to get votes here. Campaigning would be far different than we see today. This forces the politicians to pay attention to each voter and state before, during and after elections. It's clear proof of why the Electoral College needs to be eliminated.

# African Americans Do Not Trust the Federal Elections Process

## Elbert Ventura

*Elbert Ventura is a Washington, D.C.–based writer whose work has appeared in* Slate, *the* New Republic, *the* San Francisco Chronicle, *and the* Cleveland Plain Dealer, *among other outlets.*

The [2000 and 2004] presidential elections have raised serious concerns about the voting process. In 2000, the hanging chads [incompletely punched holes in paper ballots] and butterfly ballots of Florida became a symbol of flawed election technologies. In 2004, long lines and problems at the polls in predominantly black districts in Ohio raised the specter of disenfranchisement. . . .

The experience of recent years raises the question: Can Americans trust the voting system?

A study in the July 2008 issue of *The Journal of Politics* tackles that very issue. In "Are Americans Confident Their Ballots Are Counted?" authors R. Michael Alvarez, Thad E. Hall and Morgan H. Llewellyn use survey data to investigate the issue of voter confidence, which they define as the confidence the voter has that his or her vote is being counted as intended. The study finds that while the electorate in general is confident about the voting process, a crisis of confidence afflicts a segment of the voting population—a segment that is African American and Democratic.

The study used data collected from two surveys following the 2004 elections. Respondents were asked, "How confident are you that your ballot for president in the 2004 election was counted as you intended?"

The results were striking. Sixty-nine percent of whites said that they were "very confident" that their votes were counted as intended. By contrast, only 30 percent of African Americans reported that they were very confident. On the other end of the spectrum, only 8.5 percent of whites said that they were "not at all confident" or "not too confident," while 32 percent of African Americans said the same.

## Why Do Blacks Feel Less Confident?

The authors posit that the tortured history of African-American enfranchisement may have something to do with it. "[C]onfidence rates may be affected by the historical differences brought on by past efforts on the part of white voters to disenfranchise African Americans via methods such as Jim Crow laws," they write.

Problems of a more recent vintage may also play a role. Hall, an assistant professor at the University of Utah, notes that myriad problems at the polls reported in 2000 and 2004 may factor into how African Americans see the voting process.

"If you think about some of these issues and tactics that are reported in the media, they focus mainly on how it affects African Americans," Hall said. The cascade of controversies could lower black voters' confidence.

The study finds that the problem of low voter confidence isn't restricted to African Americans. Partisan affiliation seems to have an effect, too.

Comparing across white Republican and white Democratic voters, the study found that white Republicans were more likely to be very confident about their vote. The authors ascribe this to a "winner's effect." The Republican victories in 2000 and 2004, not to mention election problems with "strong partisan overtones," may have led to lower rates of confidence in the voting process among Democrats.

But the winner's effect is not static and could go the other way depending on which party wins. Alvarez, Hall and Llewellyn tested that hypothesis in a working paper published in August [2008] on the CalTech/MIT Voting Technology Project Web site investigating the effects of the 2006 midterm elections on voter confidence.

Sure enough, the study found that the Democratic takeover of the House and Senate was just the tonic for unconfident Democratic voters. "Democrats are significantly more likely relative to Republicans to increase their level of confidence following the 2006 election," the authors write. "Although Republicans are more confident than Independents and Democrats before the election, we find evidence that the confidence gap between Republicans and Democrats shrinks following the 2006 election."

The technology a voter uses also seems to have an effect on how confident they feel about their vote being counted. The study showed that those who voted using paper ballots were more confident than those who voted using punch-card, lever or touch-screen voting technologies. Absentee voters were also less trusting of the process than those who cast their votes in person.

## Not a Crisis

Despite the findings, Hall stresses that what the study found does not necessarily amount to a crisis. "In general, people's confidence is pretty high," he pointed out, even as he acknowledged that there is room for improvement. While the low level of confidence among African-American voters in particular might cause alarm, especially for the effect it might have on turnout, [the 2008] election poses an unprecedented scenario: the first African American to run for the presidency. Low confidence or not, a surge in black turnout is expected.

"If (Barack) Obama wins and if the election is problem-free, then confidence will increase markedly, among Democrats, and particularly African Americans," he predicted.

He added that a crushing Democratic win might also change how the issue of electoral reform is discussed, with progressive advocacy groups that typically champion the cause perhaps lowering the volume on their complaints and conservatives making more noise about it. . . .

---

*Those who were less confident were also less likely to vote.*

---

Asked for prescriptions on how to increase voter confidence, Hall proposed a few simple, broad fixes. "A couple of things: having good procedures in place, having transparency, having well-trained poll workers."

But perhaps just as essential is devoting more attention to the issue. The subject of voter confidence has actually been little studied by academic researchers. According to Hall, their paper is "one of the first ever written on the subject." Previous research into the issue of civic trust has focused more on trust in government—faith in democratic institutions—and not voter confidence—faith in the democratic process.

Hall said the focus on voter confidence gets to a crucial normative issue: as goes confidence, so—potentially—could go participation and legitimacy. As the authors found in a preliminary analysis, those who were less confident were also less likely to vote. "This is clearly a problem that could diminish turnout," he said.

Hall added that voter confidence touches on "a fundamental question about our democracy. We want people to be confident in how they choose their leaders."

# Poor and Minority Voters Have Historically Faced Efforts to Suppress Their Votes

*National Network for Election Reform*

*The National Network for Election Reform is a coalition of organizations that advocate for civil rights, voting rights, the disability community, students, elderly citizens, workers, nonprofits, and others.*

Our Constitutional commitment to an open and inclusive democracy is undermined by lies and tricks aimed at preventing eligible citizens from casting a ballot. Unfortunately, voters in poor and minority communities have historically faced nefarious tactics creating obstacles to effective participation in the electoral process. Forty years after the passage of the Voting Rights Act, voters across the country continue to be targets of deceptive practices and intimidation. In the years since Bull Conner [an Alabama police official whose opposition to racial integration made him a symbol of bigotry] those who wish to intimidate voters have turned to more sophisticated and nuanced devices to fraudulently prevent turnout in targeted communities. Those who perpetuate these tactics are trying to win elections through fraud instead of through the democratic process.

## Tactics Reported in 2006 Elections

- *Intimidating and deceiving Latino voters*: In Orange County, California, a congressional campaign sent 14,000 voters with Hispanic surnames a letter advising

*National Network for Election Reform*, The National Campaign for Fair Elections, 2006. © 2006 The Lawyers' Committee for Civil Rights Under Law. Reproduced by permission.

recipients that "if you're an immigrant, voting in a federal election is a crime that can result in incarceration," or deportation. Voters at a heavily Latino polling place in Tucson, Arizona were greeted by hostile gunmen providing false information about their right to vote.

- *Harassing robo calls*: Voters in New York, Virginia, Florida and New Mexico reported receiving harassing robo (automated) calls, sometimes in the middle of the night, claiming to be from one of the candidates running for office in the area. After further investigation, it became clear that the calls were coming from that candidate's opponent.

- *Lying about party affiliation to confuse the electorate*: In Maryland, materials were distributed primarily in African American neighborhoods, falsely suggesting that Republican candidates were running as Democrats or were endorsed by Democratic leaders, causing widespread confusion.

- *Deliberately providing mis-information about registration status*: Registered voters in Virginia, Colorado, and New Mexico reported receiving phone calls in the days before the election claiming that their registrations were cancelled and that if they tried to vote they would be arrested.

- *Phone calls providing voters with false polling place information*: In states from New York to Arizona, voters received phone calls with false information about their polling places. Voters were told their polling places had been changed, when they had not, and were told to vote at often inconvenient locations that were not polling places.

- *Poll workers providing voters with false information*: Poll workers in precincts across the country wrongly informed voters that identification was required in order to vote. While some of these problems were the result of poor poll worker training, in multiple incidents poll workers explained that they were imposing this requirement on their own because it was the only way to keep non-citizens from voting.

- *Students wrongly dissuaded from voting*: As in past elections, students were dissuaded from voting at their college or university and were told they would be committing a felony or that their parents would lose a tax deduction. The constitution guarantees students an equal right to participate in an election where they go to school.

## Deceptions Reported in 2004 Elections

- *Fraudulently changing party registrations and addresses.* Over 4,000 potential voters including students at Florida State and Florida A&M universities discovered their party registrations switched and their addresses changed. Changed addresses could have barred them from voting because they would have shown up at the wrong polling place.

- *Fliers advertising the wrong election date.* In Pittsburgh, fliers printed on county letterhead stated that "due to immense voter turnout expected on Tuesday," the election had been extended: Republicans vote on November 2, [2004,] and Democrats vote on November 3, [2004]. Across the country, voters received similar fliers.

- *Bogus election regulation fliers.* In Milwaukee, Wisconsin, fliers purportedly from the "Milwaukee Black Voters League" were distributed in minority neighborhoods claiming "If you've already voted in any election this year, you can't vote in the presidential election; If anybody in your family has ever been found guilty of anything, you can't vote in the presidential election; If you violate any of these laws, you can get ten years in prison and your children will get taken away from you."

- *Letters threatening arrests.* In Charleston County, South Carolina, some voters received a letter claiming to be from the NAACP [National Association for the Advancement of Colored People] which falsely threatened voters with arrest if they went to the polls and had outstanding parking tickets and had not paid child support.

- *Fraudulent memos claiming that some registrations would be invalidated.* In Lake County, Ohio, a memo on a bogus Board of Elections letterhead was sent to county residents informing them that registrations obtained through Democratic Party and NAACP registration drives were invalid.

- *Phone calls and visitors with false information.* In the Cleveland area, some voters received phone calls incorrectly informing them that their polling place had changed; Some also had unknown visitors who illegally offered to deliver completed absentee ballots to the election office.

---

*In addition to imposing penalties and fines for knowingly deceiving eligible voters, law makers should also . . . [provide] affected communities with correct information.*

---

## Other Deceptive Practices

- *Threats of imprisonment.* In 1998, state representative Son Knon's office in South Carolina mailed over 3,000 brochures to black voters, which incorrectly informed them that "SLED [State Law Enforcement Division] agents, FBI agents, people from the Justice Department and undercover agents will be in Dillon County working this election. . . . THIS ELECTION IS NOT WORTH GOING TO JAIL!!!!!!"

- *Door-to-door campaigning to "vote at home."* In 1993, campaign workers visited homes in Latino neighborhoods of Philadelphia to convince voters to cast absentee ballots while misleading voters about the documents they were signing and the state's absentee voting laws telling voters that they could vote at home as a "new way of voting."

- *Postcards encouraging voters to discard absentee ballots.* In 1990, elderly voters in Texas, received postcards that urged them to "throw the mail ballot in the trash" and "walk proudly into the voting place . . . in honor of the many who fought and died for your right to walk into the polls," even though those who have requested an absentee ballot in Texas could not vote in person without going through a complicated procedure to cancel the absentee ballot.

## Voter Intimidation

- *Men in official attire asking voters for identification.* In 2003, men with clipboards bearing official-looking insignias and 300 cars with decals resembling those of federal agencies were dispatched in black neighborhoods in Philadelphia, to ask prospective voters for identification. In a post-election poll of 1000 African-American voters, seven percent had encountered such efforts.

- *Videotaping voters at polling places.* In 1998, Republican officials in North Carolina counties planned to videotape voters in some heavily Democratic precincts purportedly to prevent fraud.

- *FBI investigation of voters.* In 1994, purportedly linked to an investigation for church arsons in Alabama, the FBI questioned 1000 voters about possible fraud, asking many to submit handwriting samples. The resulting convictions were few, but the voter turnout was down.

## Legislative Solutions

- *Deceptive conduct as an offense.* While deceptive practices are widespread and have been going on for decades, there is no effective legal structure for punishing the perpetrators of these dirty tricks. Lawmakers may categorically proscribe deceptive practices, for instance, by imposing penalties of fine and imprisonment for knowingly deceiving any person regarding the qualifications or restrictions of voter or of the time and place an election will be held.

- *Providing effective solutions.* In addition to imposing penalties and fines for knowingly deceiving eligible voters, law makers should also institute a system for providing affected communities with correct information. This can be done through programs set up by the legislature and administered by state and local election officials.

# Republicans Have Repeatedly Used Caging to Challenge Democratic Votes

*Teresa James*

*Teresa James is a lawyer for Project Vote, an organization devoted to voter engagement and participation in low-income and minority communities.*

Recent Congressional inquiries into the firings of United States Attorneys for purportedly partisan reasons have sparked interest in the esoteric term "caging." The term drew attention after former Justice Department White House liaison Monica Goodling raised it in her May 2007 testimony to the House Judiciary Committee that is investigating the firings. Ms. Goodling testified that Tim Griffin, former interim US Attorney for Arkansas, had not been forthcoming to the committee about his involvement in "voter caging" operations when he worked for the Republican National Committee (RNC). The committee members were unfamiliar with the term and did not pursue the matter beyond asking for a definition.

Ms. Goodling responded that caging is a direct mail term, and she was correct as far as she went. The term "caging" refers to a direct mail industry practice of sending out mass mailings and culling the responses according to categories that are useful to the sender, such as positive responses, no responses, or returned mail. What the committee did not ask Ms. Goodling, and what she did not volunteer, was that caging is an important first step in challenging the eligibility of voters during a political campaign. It is a component of many

Teresa James, *Caging Democracy: A 50-Year History of Partisan Challenges to Minority Voters*, Washington, DC: Project Vote, 2007. Reproduced by permission.

Republican self-described anti-fraud campaigns that historically target heavily minority and Democratic voting populations.

## Caging and Vote Suppression

Caging in this context involves sending out non-forwardable or registered mail to targeted groups of voters and compiling "caging lists" of voters whose mail was returned for any reason. Although the National Voter Registration Act (NVRA) prohibits election officials from canceling the registration of voters merely because a single piece of mail has been returned, Republican operatives have used the lists for many years in caging operations to challenge the voting rights of thousands of minority and urban voters nationwide on the basis of returned mail alone.

---

*The Democratic Party, election experts, and civic organizations charge that the intended effect of voter caging operations is to suppress minority votes.*

---

With their caging lists in hand, Republican officials and operatives take the second step in their caging operations, using the lists as the basis for media campaigns to create the impression that the returned mail is evidence of mass voter fraud. Having raised the chimera [illusion] of a voter fraud, Republican parties and operatives move into the third phase of caging operations. Operatives use the caging lists to challenge the voting eligibility of thousands of people of color and Democrats. The caging process, couched in racially neutral terms, is described in one party campaign document under the heading, "Pre-Election Day Operations—New Registration Mailing." The use of such lists by the Republican Party to challenge voters in heavily Republican precincts has not been reported.

The Democratic Party, election experts, and civic organizations charge that the intended effect of voter caging operations is to suppress minority votes. Several court decisions and occasional public comments by Republican officials lend support to this conclusion. In response, national and state Republican party entities defend caging operations as necessary ballot security measures. At least one federal court disagrees. The RNC is bound by a U.S. District Court consent decree ordering it to obtain court approval before it engages in any type of ballot security program. Yet, Republican-led caging operations continue unabated.

---

*Republican officials, to suppress Democratic votes, have focused on clearly identifiable, often physically segregated, . . . racial and ethnic minorities.*

---

Caging operations are relevant to the US Attorney dismissals because at least three of the fired US Attorneys refused to pursue voter fraud charges that could be used by Republicans to paint Democrats as perpetrators of fraud despite being pressured to do so by Republican Congress members and officials immediately before the 2006 elections. The US Attorneys are John McKay, Western District of Washington, David Iglesias, California, and Todd Graves of the Western District of Missouri. Mr. Graves' interim successor, Bradley Schlozman, brought voter fraud charges against four former employees of a community organization in the week before the 2006 election. All three fired US Attorneys had exemplary records of service in office. The common thread in their performance was that they did not respond to external pressure to prosecute weak voter fraud cases. . . .

## Targeting Minorities

Republican officials, to suppress Democratic votes, have focused on clearly identifiable, often physically segregated, . . .

racial and ethnic minorities. Before the mid-1960s the southern Democrats were the group most actively involved in suppressing the African American vote. With the advance of the Civil Rights Movement, during the 1964 presidential campaign of Barry Goldwater, a radical change took place in United States politics. Republican conservatives adopted the "Southern strategy," in which they decided to pursue the votes of alienated white Southern Democrats and forgo competing with the opposition for the votes of African Americans following their remobilization in the Civil Rights Era. GOP [Grand Old Party, a nickname for the Republican Party] ballot security programs originated in conjunction with the GOP's Southern strategy. Some contemporary RNC and state Republican officials have even admitted, privately and publicly, that caging and similar so-called "ballot security campaigns" are intended to suppress the African American vote.

In a 1986 Louisiana caging operation, the Midwest RNC political director, Kris Wolfe sent a memo to the Southern RNC political director, Lanny Griffith, saying "I would guess this program will eliminate at least 60,000 to 80,000 folks from the rolls. . . . If it's a close race . . . this could keep the black vote down considerably." This memo, which was released during a 1986 New Jersey District Court lawsuit opposing RNC caging operations, also acknowledged that the deputy political director of the National Republican Senatorial Committee had approved the caging operation.

During a 2004 Detroit election campaign, Michigan State Representative John Pappageorge told a meeting of Oakland County Republican Party members that "if we do not suppress the Detroit vote, we're going to have a tough time in this election." Detroit's population is 83 percent African American and overwhelmingly supports Democratic candidates. Apparently unaware that profiling a minority group for voter suppression violates the Voting Rights Act (VRA), Pappageorge apologized for his comment, calling it a bad choice of words.

However, he felt that the comment was not racist. Minority vote suppression is a tactic that some Republican party officials see as perfectly legitimate. They are wrong.

Challenging an elector's right to vote on the basis of racial or ethnic profiling violates the First, 14th and 15th Amendments. In addition it violates the Voting Rights Act of 1965 (VRA), which prohibits voting practices and procedures that discriminate on the basis of race or membership in a language minority group. Section II of the VRA prohibits persons acting under color of law from refusing to permit eligible persons from exercising their right to vote.

The VRA was enacted in 1965 to do away with the Jim Crow laws that prevented African Americans and other minority groups from gaining equal access to the polls. Yet, as discussed above, a remnant of the restrictions imposed by Jim Crow legislation still exist in most states in the form of statutes that allow private citizens to challenge voter eligibility. . . .

State Republican Party members and the RNC contend that caging and challenges are necessary to combat fraud by private non-profit organizations. Such groups registered significantly more than one million new voters nationwide in minority and urban communities, particularly before the 2004 election. According to one report, approximately ten million new registrations were submitted in 2004 by larger non-profit groups alone, representing more than 20% of registration applications that year. Media campaigns, intended to give the impression that voter fraud is widespread, are a hallmark of the challenge program. The resulting sensational headlines don't reflect the facts. Actual convictions for ballot fraud are rare. Where they do occur, they are by no means the exclusive province of one particular party and they rarely relate to third party registration drives.

On the other hand, Democrats and civic organizations charge that voter challenges in targeted urban, minority areas are part of a systematic nationwide Republican effort to suppress minority and Democratic votes. The charges of voter suppression are supported by the paucity of evidence of voter fraud arising from urban voter registration drives and the blanket challenges issued by Republicans in heavily minority polling places.

Statements by Republican officials lend support to the view that the immediate impetus for recent mass challenges is the increased number of newly registered voters who don't fit the Republican demographic. James P. Trakas is one example. Trakas, a Republican Party official in Cuyahoga County, Ohio, maintained before the 2004 presidential election that challenges were in response to successful third party registration drives: "The organized left's efforts to, quote-unquote, register voters—I call them ringers—have created these problems." . . .

## Overwhelming Evidence

The evidence of Republican caging operations and the mass challenge and purge attempts that follow such operations is overwhelming. Research done by experts, civic organizations and journalists into the demographics and geographic patterns of the targeted populations establishes that Republican caging operations have profiled minority and Democratic voters for challenges.

---

*The problem of caging and blanket challenges against targeted populations will not end without effort on the part of citizens.*

---

If the Republican operations were not almost exclusively limited to Democratic and minority areas, credence might be given to Republican claims that the parties are guarding ballot integrity. In the absence of evidence that Republican organizations launch caging operations against populations that are not perceived as potential political opponents, it is difficult to give credence to such claims. Voter fraud knows no party, now or in the past.

During the last half century, the focus of Republican organizations on voter caging operations has had less to do with voter fraud and more to do with a desire to use state voter challenge statutes to suppress minority and urban votes.

There is no evidence that litigation or the unintended negative consequences of voter caging programs has dampened the enthusiasm of today's Republican leadership for caging operations or mass challenges. During an appearance on behalf of the Virginia GOP gubernatorial candidate in 2005, RNC Chairman Kenneth Mehlman vowed to "do whatever we can to help make sure Jerry Kilgore becomes the next governor of the state"—including, "having poll workers on hand to challenge voter eligibility."

The problem of caging and blanket challenges against targeted populations will not end without effort on the part of citizens. Election administrators, civic organizations, and the political parties themselves must work together to prevent wholesale disenfranchisement of voters based solely on a single piece of returned mail, an ethnic surname, or a partisan challenger's "belief" that a voter is not eligible to vote.

CHAPTER 4

# How Should the U.S. Elections System Be Reformed?

# Chapter Preface

Many people believe that the 2008 election of President Barack Obama, who championed election reform when he was in the Senate, together with the election of Democratic majorities in both the U.S. Senate and House of Representatives, may bode well for serious election reform in the United States. Such reforms could include ideas such as public financing of congressional elections, permanent and universal voter registration by state governments, mandated paper trails for electronic voting machines, and the banning of various voter suppression tactics, among others. Reform might take the form of one single piece of legislation or a series of bills.

As of mid-2009, a number of election reform bills had already been introduced in both the Senate and the House. One piece of legislation that has received a significant amount of press attention—called Fair Elections Now—was introduced in the U.S. Senate by Dick Durbin and Arlen Specter and in the U.S. House of Representatives by John Larsen and Walter Jones. If passed, this legislation would provide public funding for candidates running for Congress. Other Senate bills include Senator John Ensign's Voting Integrity and Verification Act (S. 48), a bill to require voter machines purchased after 2012 to produce voter-verifiable paper records and require manual audits of those paper votes. Another bill, the Weekend Voting Act (S. 149), introduced by Senator Herb Kohl, would establish election day as the first Saturday and Sunday after the first Friday in November, every even-numbered year. A companion bill was introduced in the House—H.R. 354 by Steve Israel and one cosponsor.

Meanwhile, Senate Joint Resolution 4, introduced by Ben Nelson, would abolish the Electoral College and provide for the popular election of the president and vice-president. A similar bill in the House (H.R. 9) was introduced by Gene

Green. Senate Joint Resolution 7, sponsored by Russ Feingold and two other senators, would require the popular election of Senators who fill Senate vacancies (instead of the current system, which allows state governors to appoint a replacement). In addition, Senator Joe Lieberman, together with thirteen other sponsors, introduced S. 160, the District of Columbia Voting Rights Act, to provide the District of Columbia with a voting seat in the U.S. House of Representatives. The companion bill in the House (H.R. 157) was introduced by Eleanor Norton and two cosponsors. Another House bill, H.R. 655, from Dana Rohrabacker, would treat District of Columbia residents as residents of Maryland for purpose of voting for congressional and presidential elections.

Members of the House of Representatives have proposed additional reforms. John Conyers, for example, introduced several notable bills. One is the Caging Prohibition Act (H.R. 103), which would prohibit election officials from preventing individuals from voting based on challenges to eligibility derived from voter caging lists—that is, lists compiled when voters fail to respond to direct mailings that are then used to suppress voting. In addition, Conyers and eighteen cosponsors introduced the Deceptive Practices and Voter Intimidation Prevention Act (H.R. 97), aimed at other voter suppression activities—such as the knowing communication of false information about the time, place, or conduct of elections; challenges to voter eligibility; and explicit endorsements of candidates for office—with the intention of preventing people from voting in elections. Another piece of legislation introduced by Conyers, along with five cosponsors, is the Voting Opportunity and Technology Enhancement Rights Act (H.R. 105)—a bill that provides for a variety of election reforms, among them: write-in absentee ballots, voter-verifiable records for all voting systems, the counting of provisional ballots, election day registration, early voting, online voter registration, and voting rights for persons with criminal records. A related bill is Representative Sheila Jackson-Lee's Ex-offenders Voting Rights Act (H.R. 59), which gives the right to vote to persons who have completed terms of imprisonment for felony convictions.

Other bills in the House include the Let the People Decide Clean Campaign Act (H.R. 158), introduced by David Obey and six cosponsors to establish spending limits for House races and provide public funding for candidates' expenditures. A bill from Alcee Hastings and five cosponsors, the Critical Election Infrastructure Act (H.R. 153), would make grants to the states to train election officials, buy election equipment, hire more election officials, and improve elections. Another bill from Representative Hastings, the American Elections Act (H.R. 764), would require that ballots and voting information for federal elections be provided in English only. House Resolution 13, introduced by Marcy Kaptur and one cosponsor, attempts to amend the Constitution to give Congress and the states the power to set contribution limits on campaign spending. Finally, House Resolution 2, introduced by Donna Christensen, would amend the Constitution to prevent the right to vote from being abridged on account of residency.

Many commentators suggest, however, that the best way to achieve needed election reform is to develop a core agenda of reforms that can be solidified into a unified, comprehensive piece of legislation that could win broad support, both in Congress and among voters. Whether President Obama and Congress will focus on this issue amid the many other pressing national crises and successfully develop and pass either partial or comprehensive election reform during the next several months or years, remains to be seen. The authors of the viewpoints in this chapter discuss this idea of comprehensive reform as well as various other reform proposals.

# State Election Officials Should Restore Trust in Voter Registration

## Christian Science Monitor

*The* Christian Science Monitor *is an international daily newspaper published in the United States.*

Since the "hanging chad" [incompletely punched holes in paper ballots] debacle of 2000, states have worked hard to restore trust in Election Day by updating voting machines. Slowly, but surely, they're making progress. But now, charges of "fraud" and "suppression" in voter registration are kicking up a cloud of controversy—and again endangering voter confidence.

As with financial markets, so with the voting process: the integrity of the system is critical to making it work. Places such as Florida's Palm Beach County may be on their third set of machines in three elections, but at least they're going at their equipment problems until they get it right. Several high-profile cases [in the 2008] campaign season, though, show that the country also needs to get it right with people.

---

*No-match rejection is a greater threat to voting integrity [than fraud] because common technical mistakes, such as name misspellings, could affect thousands of people.*

---

Republicans are all over an activist group called ACORN [Association of Community Organizations for Reform Now], some of whose workers have recorded thousands of fraudulent names during a massive voter registration drive. Bogus

ACORN lists turned up in registrar offices in about a dozen states. The FBI is reportedly investigating. Democrats have their own complaints. In battleground states such as Ohio and Minnesota, they accuse Republicans of voter suppression for questioning names of newly registered voters whose identifying information doesn't match what's in state databases.

As part of the Help America Vote Act of 2002, Congress required states to centralize voter lists, which allows voters to check their registration and polling places online. If there's a no-match of new voters with, say, Social Security or driver's license records, states must notify these voters and give them a chance to prove eligibility—but this isn't always carried out.

Four states require election officials to reject no-match registrations. Lawsuits to copy these rules are under way in three other states.

In practice, no-match rejection is a greater threat to voting integrity because common technical mistakes, such as name misspellings, could affect thousands of people. Of over 20,000 failed matches in Florida, for instance, more than three-quarters were due to typos. About 200,000 no-match names are being legally challenged in Ohio—more than the vote by which George Bush beat John Kerry in 2004.

---

*The country should start to debate the idea of "universal voter registration."*

---

It's more difficult for registration fraud to turn into voter fraud. "Mickey Mouse," as was registered with ACORN, is unlikely to show up at your local polling station. There were only 38 cases of federal prosecutions of illegal voting between 2002 and 2005.

## Rethinking Voter Registration

Both the fraud and suppression charges undermine voter confidence. This is not the first time ACORN has come under fire, and it needs to clean up its act. Likewise, state election officials need to solve the no-match problem.

Beyond this, the country should start to debate the idea of "universal voter registration."

In most advanced democracies, governments—not groups such as ACORN—automatically register citizens to vote. It is still up to individuals to exercise this most basic right, but it is not nearly so difficult to get it as in the United States, where 30 percent of Americans are not registered to vote, according to the 2006 Census.

It could be that a rethink of registration may be next on America's to-do list to shore up voter confidence.

# Universal Voter Registration Is Urgently Needed

## Election Protection

*Election Protection is a nonpartisan voter protection and education group formed to ensure that all voters had an equal opportunity to participate in the 2008 elections.*

The 2008 election was just another illustration of what makes our democratic system so great—millions of voters streaming to the polling place regardless of age, race, income or level of education. Unfortunately, the news wasn't all good. Voters across the country arrived at the polls to find that their registrations had never been processed, that their names had been purged from voter lists, or that they had missed the registration deadlines altogether.

Fortunately, there is a solution to the problem—Voter Registration Modernization. Since the [2008] election, many leading voices in our nation have spoken out about the urgent need to update our antiquated registration system. The Senate Rules Committee held a hearing on March 11th [2009] to discuss problems with our voter registration system where Election Protection's Jonah Goldman testified, saying, "Each election the voter registration system, this relic of the country's pre–Civil War past, blocks millions of eligible Americans from casting a ballot, distracts election officials from performing critical administrative tasks, and needlessly wastes millions of critical dollars at a time when state and local budgets are stretching every penny. Congress has the power and the opportunity to modernize this system." . . .

In addition to ensuring that no eligible American gets turned away because her name is not on the rolls, updating our registration system will relieve this sometimes overwhelming burden of voter registration on election officials. Removing this weight will allow those election officials to focus on the other problems that block eligible voters from exercising their right to vote.

## Newspaper Editorials

The *New York Times* published an editorial, "Still Broken," on March 17th [2009], reminding us that "supporters of a more fair, efficient and inclusive system of voting should not let this moment slip away":

> The most important change Congress can make is to require universal voter registration. That would put the burden on states to register eligible voters—identifying them from other government lists such as tax and motor vehicle databases—rather than forcing prospective voters to navigate the obstacle-ridden path to the voting rolls. States should also be required to make registration permanent so voters are not purged from the rolls because of a move to a new address or a name change.
>
> Congress should enact lenient federal rules for voter identification, allowing voters to present a wide array of IDs. Far too many states have onerous requirements that make it particularly hard for poor people and racial minorities to vote. And it should outlaw vote suppression and other campaign dirty tricks.

On March 16th [2009] the *Washington Post* called on Congress to modernize our registration system in an editorial, "Shut Out at the Polls":

> ... the cumbersome, paper-based system of voter registration needs to be overhauled. Not only is it the prime reason that many voters are blocked from casting ballots, but it diverts local election officials from more critical tasks such as training poll workers or processing absentee ballots. Voting

rights advocates make a strong case for shifting the onus for registration from voters to the state, using technology and existing databases (such as tax records and motor vehicle lists) to build a permanent roster. Voters should have a convenient way of verifying that they are properly registered, and there is no reason that they should lose their right to vote simply because they move to another block or state or change their names.

---

*A number of newspaper articles highlighted the need for Registration Modernization.*

---

In a March 11th [2009] op-ed in *Roll Call*, "Voter Registration System Needs to Be Modernized," Robin Carnahan, the Democratic Secretary of State for Missouri, and Trey Grayson, the Republican Secretary of State for Kentucky, encouraged the Senate Rules Committee "in a bipartisan way, to consider the challenges of our [voter registration] system and ways in which its efficiency, accuracy and cost effectiveness can be improved":

> We must significantly streamline voter registration and make greater use of technology to weed out inefficiencies. Right now, many voters have no convenient way of verifying that they're on the rolls, or that their information is accurate, leading them to submit duplicate registrations to ensure their right to vote is secure. If voters move between states or within a state, or, even more simply, change their name, their old, outdated registration record often remains for several years. Simplifying and automating the process could help save time and money and, most importantly, protect voters.

A few days after the election, on November 9th [2008], the *Washington Post* spoke out for Registration Modernization in an editorial, "A Better Vote":

> It's time to rethink another vestige of an earlier era—a voter registration system that not only prevents people from vot-

ing but causes myriad troubles for election officials. Without question, the biggest headaches this past election stemmed from voters wrongly purged from state rolls or election offices swamped with fraudulent applications. There's a growing clamor by voting rights advocates to shift the onus on registering from the individual to government. Not only would this remove the single biggest obstacle to voting (consider that in 2004, 28 percent of eligible Americans were not registered to vote), but it would make manipulation of the system harder.

## A Need for Modernization

A number of newspaper articles highlighted the need for Registration Modernization. The *National Journal* published an online article by David Hebert with the headline, "The Morning After, Voting Problems Remain." Hebert observed EP [Election Protection] headquarters in action on November 4th [2008], where volunteers worked tirelessly to help voters at the polls. On Election Day, EP's Jonah Goldman, director of the National Campaign for Fair Elections, acknowledged the need for reform so that Election Protection does not have "to be here in two or four years." The article discusses the effectiveness of previous reform like the Help America Vote Act, citing EP's Jon Greenbaum, director of the Voting Rights Project at the Lawyers' Committee for Civil Rights Under Law [a pro-voting legal group], who told Hebert, "You pass legislation that has a lot of problems, and then you create a commission that doesn't have any teeth. . . . It doesn't get listened to very much." Hebert describes Election Protection's goals for electoral change:

> The Election Protection groups' ultimate goal, organizers said, is to help pass legislation currently being crafted in the House and Senate that would automatically register eligible voters nationwide and mandate that all states provide early voting options.

The article also includes a link to "An Election Reformer's Wish List," another piece by Hebert which details some of the reform suggestions Voting Rights Groups advocate.

On November 6, 2008, the *New York Times* published an article by Ian Urbina titled, "Push to Expand Voter Rolls and Early Balloting in U.S." In the article, former Senator Hillary Rodham Clinton is quoted as saying:

> A system of automatic registration, in which the government bears more of the responsibility for assembling accurate and secure lists of eligible voters, is a necessary reform. . . . All eligible Americans should be able to cast their ballot without barriers, and the registration problems we saw on [Election Day] and during the weeks that preceded Election Day make clear that the system needs improvement.

Rosemary E. Rodriguez, chair of the federal Election Assistance Commission, said:

> The single most important thing that Congress can do right now is create universal voter registration, which would mean that all eligible voters are automatically registered.

---

*Election reformers are calling for a move toward a "universal voter registration" system, in which the government [ensures] . . . that all eligible citizens are registered to vote.*

---

On November 7, 2008, *USA Today* published an article from Richard Wolf, "Election Gives Early-Balloting Initiatives a Boost," that discussed the momentum the 2008 elections provided for election reform.

> Besides lines, the biggest problems [on Election Day] had to do with voter-registration systems. Even with new electronic databases, states often dropped would-be voters from their rolls if their names or data didn't match driver's or Social Security records.

That has led advocacy groups to push for universal registration—a system used by at least 24 other countries in which all eligible citizens are automatically able to vote and permanently kept on the rolls.

In addition to Registration Modernization, the article also mentioned improving election administration, banning deceptive practices, and early voting as important pieces of reform.

In a *Los Angeles Times* article, "Voter Registration Process Is under Scrutiny," David G. Savage wrote:

> The nation's much-maligned election system passed a major test last week when more than 132 million Americans—a record—cast ballots with few reports of problems. But now, election reformers are calling for a move toward a 'universal voter registration' system, in which the government takes the lead in ensuring that all eligible citizens are registered to vote.

Savage went on to quote Wendy R. Weiser from Election Protection coalition partner the Brennan Center as saying, "This means the registration process would no longer serve as a barrier to the right to vote."

# The Presidential Primary Process Should Be Reformed

*Adam Graham*

*Adam Graham was Montana state coordinator for the Alan Keyes campaign in 2000, and in 2004 was a candidate for the Republican nomination for the governor of Idaho. He writes about U.S. and Idaho politics and hosts a political podcast, "The Truth and Hope Report."*

There seems to be growing consensus around the need to reform the Presidential nominating process. Few like the way our current system works, and there are a wide range of proposals to change it.

The problem is that while we agree on our dislike of the current system, we disagree on how to fix it, or even what the problem is. Some of the solutions proposed are imperious at best: trying to make every detail of our primary system perfect. One proposal I read wanted to reform everything down to the details of who moderates the debates.

The saying KISS (Keep It Simple, Stupid) applies to reforming the nominating process. The more details, the more areas addressed, the more complexity added in, the more people you need on board, the less chance you're going to get something done.

## The Problems

In an interview with Stateline at the National Governors Association, Mississippi Governor and Former RNC [Republican National Committee] Chairman Haley Barbour defined the problem in two words: "Frontloading" and "Compression."

What do these forces do? If you like the idea of political ads running around Christmas, Presidential Debates being held April of the year before the election, and campaigns that require hundreds of fundraisers and $60 million to run, then you love frontloading and compression. If you like Presidential Campaigns ending as result of a non-binding straw poll held in August the year before the election, this is a great process. If you think it's great for our Republic that [2008's] GOP [Grand Old Party, a nickname for the Republican Party] nomination is decided before voters in 11 states with a combined population of 42.1 million Americans went to the polls, then our current process is wonderful. And if we keep it up, [Representative] Duncan Hunter's announcement [that] he was running for president two years before the election is held may seem like a late date to start in a few years.

*Some people would like to do away with caucuses. Yet others . . . feel the caucus system is superior.*

These two issues must be addressed. Other issues are comparatively unimportant and some people should be left alone.

Some people would like to do away with caucuses. Yet others like myself feel the caucus system is superior. Still, many in states across our country know the caucus system is far less expensive than holding a presidential primary that may or may not matter, and preferable to not having a voice in the process at all. Let the people of the several states address this, because they're the ones who pay for these contests.

## Alternatives

Many people think that a national primary is a solution. However, it solves nothing. A National Primary would make presidential campaigns more expensive and the process would be just as long as it is today. A National Primary is the ultimate of compression and frontloading combined.

Either the Delaware system or rotating regional primaries would solve the problems with our current frontloaded process by spreading out states on the basis of size (from smallest to largest) or geography. Both are excellent plans, both however would be hard to pass.

The Delaware Plan would face resistance from large states. Would California, New York, Florida, Texas, and Pennsylvania really agree to be in the last group of states to vote? The Rotating Regional plan would run into resistance from many states that simply didn't want to do it.

Any of the major reform plans face major challenges. How are you going to force states to participate? A federal law? A party edict? Who is going to fund these primaries? Stripping all delegates from a state hasn't exactly worked very well for Democrats this time around. What else can they try? The Republicans' plan of taking away half the delegates until the nominee (like an irresponsible parent) gives them back?

In addition, particularly on the Republican side, many people have a sense of federalism and believe each state should decide the timing of its own contest for itself. How exactly do you force a system on all the states from on high?

## A Market Solution

There's an incentive to move your primary up, but no incentive to vote later in the process. States that move up get to claim more influence over the process. States that don't get nothing other than saving the cost of holding a special election.

---

*If you change party rules so that states that hold early contests are able to award fewer pledged delegates, states that vote later will have a greater influence on the process.*

---

The reason states hold early primaries is so that they can get influence. States can influence presidential politics in two ways. The first is through the momentum they provide a winning candidate and the second is through the pledged delegates they allot.

A pledged delegate is required to vote for a candidate on the first ballot at the national convention, and ultimately winning a majority of the delegates is what the campaign is all about.

So thus, if you change party rules so that states that hold early contests are able to award fewer pledged delegates, states that vote later will have a greater influence on the process. I don't favor taking delegates away from states, but rather, based on when the election is held, only a certain percent of delegates will be pledged and any delegates beyond an allowed percentage are elected at the State Convention as Uncommitted, Unpledged Delegates that can vote however they wish on the convention floor. So, these elected delegates will be free agents.

I would propose the following system:

If your state holds its Primary or Caucus before January 15, it cannot award any pledged delegates. If your state holds its Primary or Caucus before February 15, it can award 25% of its delegates as pledged. If your state holds its primary before March 15, it can award 50% of its delegates as pledged. If your state holds its primary before April 15, it can award 75% of its delegates pledged. If your state holds it primary on or after April 15, all of its delegates can be awarded as pledged.

Now, it should be noted that this is not the same as the Super Delegate concept. Super Delegates are party bosses who are guaranteed a vote at the convention no matter what. Unpledged delegates would be elected by party members at a convention and entrusted with judgment over the presidential race at the convention.

If this became the policy of political parties, states that have moved up their primaries for presidential influence will have to decide how they want to influence the process. Some will opt to keep their primaries where they are in order to offer momentum to candidates. However, I sort of doubt that California wants to elect 127 unpledged Republican delegates to the national convention, so they would probably move their primary back. Perhaps, you would have a Super Tuesday around Mid-April, but it would not be nearly as packed, because many states would still choose to go in February and March to get more influence despite the loss of pledged delegates. Because of the number of Uncommitted Delegates elected, there would be a greater chance that later states like North Carolina, Indiana, and Idaho would still have a voice in the process by the time the issue reached them.

There are plans that, if implemented, would work as well as this, perhaps better. The problem is that there are many hurdles that over the past eight years have proven almost impossible to get over. And we must do something before we find ourselves in another out of control election.

# Electronic Voting Systems Can Be Further Improved

## Grant Gross

*Grant Gross is Washington, D.C., correspondent for IDG News Service, covering legislation and regulation related to technology and telecommunications.*

[The 2008] U.S. election may not be long remembered for widespread problems with voting systems, but there were at least scattered reports of problems with touch-screen or optical-scan voting machines, many compounded by record turnouts in some jurisdictions.

Amid those scattered, if not widespread, reports of problems with electronic voting, critics of e-voting machines said there's still work that can be done to improve the voting process and voting technology. And the nation's top election official said she's confident that voting systems can be improved and that elections can run more smoothly.

### Certification of Voting Machines

The U.S. Elections Assistance Commission (EAC), established by the 2002 Help America Vote Act (HAVA), hopes to start certifying e-voting machines [in 2009], said Rosemary Rodriguez, chairwoman of the EAC. The EAC launched a new program to certify the integrity of e-voting machines early in 2007, and some e-voting machine vendors have complained that the commission is moving too slowly to certify machines.

Six e-voting vendors have pending applications for certification, with the earliest application in February 2007, and the EAC hasn't yet certified any of them. But Rodriguez said the EAC is taking its time to make sure its certification program is extensive and focused on the right things. "We're not going to apologize for being thorough," Rodriguez said in an interview.

There were early reports of voting machine breakdowns in Michigan, Ohio, Pennsylvania and New Jersey, with touch-screen machines having problems in some areas and optical-scan machines with problems in other areas. There were also reports of voter databases not being up to date in Ohio and other states.

Generally, local voting officials seem to have been prepared for large turnouts and potential problems, Rodriguez said. However, there is room for improvement, and one of the EAC's focuses will be on voting machine certification, she said.

It may not be realistic to "expect perfection," she said. "It may never be perfect, but it will not be for lack of trying on our part."

E-voting vendors played down the reports of machine problems [on Election Day 2008]. "It is an exceedingly quiet day for our team," said Michelle Shafer, vice president of communications and external affairs at Sequoia Voting Systems.

---

*The U.S. needs "fully tested voting machines that reliably perform their functions, backup plans and well-trained poll workers."*

---

Some election observers seem to want a level of perfection that's not possible, added David Beirne, executive director of the Election Technology Council, a trade group representing e-voting vendors.

"We are not seeing widespread problems with any of the voting machines themselves," he said. "Every election is going to have its own individual challenges, but today's election [in 2008] is performing very well regardless of the doomsday expectations bantered about within the press. One thing to point out is that a few reports have focused on issues that pertain to the ballot layout and setup of contests rather than the performance of the machines themselves."

Asked if Congress should enact new standards for e-voting, Beirne disagreed. First, the EAC needs to act on the certification applications it has, he said.

"Congress and policy-makers can adopt as many requirements for standards as they like, but until such time that they recognize the challenges the industry is facing with our ability to certify current product upgrades, it makes no difference how many versions of new voting system standards are mandated if we are unable to bring those new products to the marketplace," Beirne said.

## Major Changes Needed

Brian Chess, chief scientist at software security vendor Fortify Software Inc., disagreed, saying the U.S. still needs to make major changes. The U.S. needs "fully tested voting machines that reliably perform their functions, backup plans and well-trained poll workers," he said. "We are already hearing about unreliable machines, both DRE [direct-recording electronic], and optical scan, failing and causing long lines."

Chess called on Congress to pass "strict national standards on security" for e-voting machines. "We need to test ways the machines could fail and the reliability of the machines in a true election environment," he said. "We also need to write the standards to make the vendors responsible for the behavior of their machines, including the off-the-shelf components . . . and when procedures break down."

Those standards need to be binding, he added. "No voting machine that fails to meet them should be used to cast a vote for our president."

The real question is whether fixing voting systems will be a top priority, even with "quite a few" reports of voting problems [in 2008] . . . , said longtime e-voting critic Eugene Spafford, chairman of the U.S. Public Policy Committee of the Association for Computing Machinery. "The question comes down to, how much are we willing to spend, and how confident do we want to be in the results?" said Spafford, a computer science professor at Purdue University.

---

*In the rush to adopt new voting technology following problems with paper ballots in the 2000 elections, many states adopted unproven technology.*

---

In some cases ..., problems with optical-scan machines seemed to be connected to rain. Voters brought moisture into the polling places and the optical-scan machines jammed because of damp paper, he said. In other places, voters raised questions because their ballots were put in boxes waiting to be scanned instead of scanned immediately, he said.

Those problems may have been predictable, but a lot of the problems center around training of poll workers, many of whom aren't familiar with the technology, Spafford said. More extensive training will cost money.

In other cases, any problems with voting machinery were compounded by record voter turnouts. Several states have moved to allow early voting, and other states may want to consider it, Spafford said.

In the rush to adopt new voting technology following problems with paper ballots in the 2000 elections, many states adopted unproven technology, he added. While most states that purchased touch-screen voting machines have since moved to include printouts with those machines, other states have switched to optical-scan machines.

Three states—Maryland, Tennessee and Colorado—will move to some kind of paper backup in coming elections. But that still leaves 15 states where touch-screen machines would be used without paper backups, and replacing or reconfiguring those machines would cost millions of dollars.

The U.S. government is facing major challenges in coming years, even if Democrats generally sympathetic to voting reform issues add to their majorities in Congress, Spafford said. "We have so many other pressing national concerns that are going to require attention first," he said. "We have so many issues, I wonder whether this will bubble up high enough to get addressed soon. It needs addressing."

# The Electoral College System Should Be Reformed by Adopting the National Popular Vote Plan

*Jamin Raskin*

*Jamin Raskin is a professor of constitutional law at American University and a Democratic state senator in Maryland. He introduced the National Popular Vote plan that was signed into law by Maryland's governor on April 10, 2007.*

It's hardly news at this point that, as it works today, the Electoral College undermines American democracy. It does so in three fundamental ways: First, it betrays the principle of majority rule, threatening every four years to deliver the White House to the popular-vote loser. Second, it reduces the general election contest to a matter of what happens in Ohio, Florida, and a handful of other swing states, leaving most Americans (who live in forsaken "red" and "blue" states) on the sidelines. This in turn depresses turnout and helps give us one of the worst rates of voter participation on earth. Third, because of its proven pliability, the Electoral College invites partisan operatives, legislators, secretaries of state and even Supreme Court justices to engage in constant strategic mischief and manipulation at the state level.

## Partisan Proposals

This last problem is about to make things much worse, as strategic actors try to exploit spreading discontent with the system by pushing "reform" proposals for purely partisan advantage. Thus, in California, top Republican strategists are now proposing a ballot initiative that would "reform" the system by awarding the state's electoral votes by congressional district. Its real purpose is to break up the state's 55 electors, which typically go to the Democrats in a bloc as inevitably as Texas, Georgia, and Oklahoma give their 56 combined electors to the Republicans. Following the proposed division of California's well-gerrymandered [voting districts divided in such as way as to influence voting outcomes] blue and red congressional districts, it is likely that the 2008 GOP [Grand Old Party, a nickname for the Republican Party] nominee under this plan would carry away about 20 electors. In one fell swoop, this would ruin the Democrats' chances for winning the presidency.

This is very plainly not reform. It is tactical gamesmanship. . . .

---

*The National Popular Vote plan . . . simply benefits that party whose presidential candidate best appeals to the majority of Americans in an election.*

---

## The National Popular Vote Plan

Citizens who are truly serious about transforming the Electoral College actually have a sturdy nonpartisan vehicle by which to move us to the kind of popular presidential election that citizens in nearly every other democracy enjoy. We don't need a new partisan trick to "fix" our presidential process. We need only enact the existing obvious solution.

The "National Popular Vote" plan, which is on the table in 47 states, has been signed into law in Maryland and had actually passed *both* houses in California in 2006 before it was vetoed by Gov. Arnold Schwarzenegger. It simply calls for an interstate compact among all states to agree to cast their electoral votes for the winner of the national popular vote. It becomes effective and binding when states representing at least 270 electors enter the compact. This is the way we will get to elect presidents as we elect governors and senators: everyone acting together, without games and subterfuge.

The plan has the backing of distinguished Republican statesmen like former Utah Sen. Jake Garn, former Minnesota Sen. David Durenberger, former Illinois Rep. John Anderson, former Alabama Rep. John Buchanan, and former California Rep. Tom Campbell, as well as distinguished Democrats like former Indiana Sen. Birch Bayh, and former New York Rep. Tom Downey. It has been endorsed by newspapers from the *New York Times* and *Minneapolis Star-Tribune* to the *Los Angeles Times* and *Sacramento Bee.*

---

*It is time for the American people to elect the president directly and democratically.*

---

## Republican Opposition

As far as I can tell, the only thing the plan lacks is active support from Republicans in office. Indeed, for some reason, there is a constant undertow of opposition from the party. I know this because when I introduced the plan in the Maryland Senate, I had expressions of enthusiasm from several Republican colleagues, one of whom even voted for it in committee. But when it came to the floor, all of the Republicans voted against it. They claimed that it would hurt small states even though small states that are safely red or blue—like Rhode Island or Montana—are ignored today just like the large ones (such as New York or Texas). They said that we should stick with the handiwork of the Framers—even though the current Electoral College process is distant from the way it was practiced in the 18th century and even though the Constitution clearly empowers the states to appoint electors as we see fit, including on the basis of the national popular vote. On the House side, only one Republican supported the bill. It passed with overwhelming (but not unanimous) Democratic support.

We Maryland Democrats were not acting in a partisan spirit. The National Popular Vote plan will not necessarily help (or hurt) us. In small-*d* democratic fashion, it simply benefits that party whose presidential candidate best appeals to the majority of Americans in an election—that could be us or them. Several colleagues pointed out to me that, had John Kerry won another 60,000 votes in Ohio, he would have prevailed in the Electoral College but still lost the national popular vote by more than 3 million votes. My answer then was: So be it. The object here is not to get a Democrat elected president. It's to get the person with the most votes elected. Is democracy itself now a partisan idea?

The current system is arbitrary, accident-prone, and increasingly untenable. On that I can agree with the Republicans who back the California initiative. What I cannot accept is that a more convoluted system, undertaken by a single state for transparently political reasons, is the solution. It is time for the American people to elect the president directly and democratically. Let us give every American incentive to vote in an election in which every vote counts. Let us (finally) agree to stop playing strategic games and let the chips fall where they may with a national popular vote.

Thomas Jefferson famously said: "We are all republicans, we are all federalists." Today, at least for the purposes of creating a national election for president in which every vote counts equally, we should all be Republicans and Democrats, Independents and Greens and Libertarians. Why not put aside political party just for a moment to see if we can still work together to create a more perfect union?

# The National Popular Vote Plan Is a Bad Idea

*Mathew J. Franck*

*Mathew J. Franck is a professor and chairman of the Political Science Department at Radford University in Virginia, where he has taught American politics, constitutional law, and political philosophy since 1989. He is also the author of several books.*

In [the December 15, 2008,] *Wall Street Journal*, Jonathan Soros writes that "It's Time to Junk the Electoral College." I have no doubt that the electoral college will survive this latest assault, but bad arguments ought to be slapped down anyway—especially on the very day when the electors meet in their state capitals to cast their official ballots.

## A Bad Solution

Soros backs an idea first floated by the Brothers Amar (law professors Akhil and Vikram), which would undo the electoral college but not by amending the Constitution to eliminate it. Instead, state legislatures (responsible for legislating the manner in which presidential electors are chosen) would write statutes that would award their electoral votes to the party whose candidate won a nationwide popular-vote majority. So, for instance, if a Republican won nationally but lost badly in New York, and New York's state legislature had written such a law, the state's electoral votes would go Republican even though more New Yorkers had voted Democratic.

Since no state legislature wants to jump off this cliff unless everyone else jumps too, each state that passes such legislation would make its operation contingent on the enactment by enough of the rest of the states to make a total of 270 elec-

Mathew J. Franck, "Junk Arguments Against the Electoral College," *National Review Online*, December 15, 2008. Copyright © 2008 by National Review, Inc., 215 Lexington Avenue, New York, NY 10016. Reproduced by permission.

toral votes, or a majority in the college. If that threshold were reached, the practice of the remaining states wouldn't matter, since the states in the so-called "National Popular Vote Compact" would control the outcome. (Of course the votes of citizens everywhere would continue to matter, since the decisive thing would be a national tally of the popular vote.)

---

*The electoral college with the winner-take-all rule in (most of) the states is perfectly democratic. It's just federally democratic, rather than being nationally democratic.*

---

This idea is a solution in search of a problem. Soros identifies just two reasons to adopt this proposal. The first is that the current winner-take-all practice (in effect in 48 states) leads candidates to campaign only in competitive states, and to ignore states safely in either camp. The second reason is that once in a while the winner of the nationally aggregated popular vote is not the winner of the election, as happened in 2000.

Take the second reason first. Soros does not even attempt to argue that an occasional burp, in which the winner of the electoral college majority is not the winner of a national popular vote plurality, is an injustice. Maybe he regards it as self-evidently undemocratic, but it's not. The electoral college with the winner-take-all rule in (most of) the states is perfectly democratic. It's just federally democratic, rather than being nationally democratic. What is needed (and never provided by electoral college critics) is an argument why we should prefer the undifferentiated aggregate majority rule of the nation's voters to the differentiated and segmented majority rule of the states' voters.

Also, as many people have pointed out (including me on previous occasions), the current arrangement has the advantage of confining recount contests within the bounds of particular states. Any election in which the "wrong" candidate wins the electoral-vote majority will very probably be a quite close election nationally—as was 2000. Controversies over counts and recounts will at least occur in just one or a few states (e.g., Florida [in 2000]), rather than in thousands of precincts in all 50 states. [In 2008] it was some days before the state of Missouri was sure which candidate would receive its electoral votes. Take that problem national in a close election, and think about the nightmare of delays and the crisis of legitimacy that might result.

---

*In any electoral environment, the candidates' resources will go wherever the payoff is likely to be greatest.*

---

Soros's other argument is that [in 2008], for instance, the two major candidates "devoted more than 98% of their television ad spending and campaign events to just 15 states which together make up about a third of the U.S. population." (I'm not sure I trust that 98% figure, but let that go.) In any electoral environment, the candidates' resources will go wherever the payoff is likely to be greatest—and that means slighting the scenes of victories you can take for granted as much as those where your defeat is assured. So where would candidates' resources be more efficiently expended in an electoral environment in which only the national popular vote mattered?

Most likely, we would see campaigning in urban centers and vote-rich near suburbs. The northeast corridor (D.C. to Boston), the great cities of the West and Gulf coasts and the Great Lakes (from San Diego to Seattle, from Mobile to Houston, and from Buffalo to Milwaukee)—many of them taken for granted in recent elections—would suddenly become relevant, and would remain permanently so as long as they retained their prominence as dense population centers. Some of the great river cities on the Missouri and Mississippi and Ohio might get some attention too. Advertising in and candidate travel to these rich seams of votes would be the order of the day. Oh, and has anyone noticed that most of them are biased heavily to the Democratic Party? I'm sure that has nothing to do with the proposal's popularity. Who would lose out? The states and localities in flyover country—the rural areas, the small towns, the more culturally conservative parts of the country.

Soros complains that only one third of the states were paid any attention in the recent campaign. Does anyone think that candidates would show up in more of the country under his proposal?

Think again of the permanent importance of this bias toward the urban and against the rural. One of the interesting things about our current system is that it doesn't stand still. Anyone old enough to remember Ronald Reagan can recall when California was a state Republicans sometimes won. One day it will be again. So complaints that candidates only go to one third of the country ring hollow when we reflect that over time there is considerable change in *which* third of the country is most heavily targeted by candidates. Any state feeling slighted today need only become more competitive between the parties—something one of the parties surely wants in every one of those states—to change its fortunes in the next presidential election. But under Soros's idea the geography of presidential campaigning would follow the iron law of population density. Movement over time would occur glacially by comparison.

## A Harebrained Idea

Maryland, New Jersey, Illinois, and Hawaii are so far the only states to pass the legislation desired by Soros and friends. Each one is, lately, a predictably Democratic state. Not so long ago Illinois was a battleground, and if it becomes one again it will probably have the good sense to repeal this foolish legislation.

A last problem with the "compact" is that if it really is a compact among the states concerned, it appears to violate Article I, section 10 of the Constitution: "No State shall, without the Consent of Congress . . . enter into any Agreement or Compact with another State . . ." Do Soros et al. plan to push a bill in Congress that would permit the states to do this? One might say it is no true "compact" at all since it entails each state merely exercising its independent Article II power to say how its electors will be chosen. But the conditioning of each state law's operation on the choice of other states to do likewise may make this an unconstitutional compact.

I don't think this could be effectively challenged in any court, but I also don't think it will ever reach that point. The four states mentioned above provide fewer than one fifth of the votes needed to make this scheme effective. And too few of the other 46 states, I'm sure, will find it in their interest or their country's interest to pursue this harebrained idea.

# The United States Should Pursue Comprehensive Election Reform

*Wendy R. Weiser and Jonah Goldman*

*Wendy R. Weiser is director of the Democracy Project of the Brennan Center for Justice at New York University School of Law, and Jonah Goldman is director of the National Campaign for Fair Elections in the Lawyers' Committee for Civil Rights Under Law's Voting Rights Project.*

Our Constitution promises every eligible American a full and equal opportunity to participate in the political process. Unfortunately, defects in election administration and procedures undermine that promise by disenfranchising countless eligible Americans every election cycle. These defects can be remedied, and the promise of democracy restored, by implementing real reforms to ensure that all eligible Americans have a fair and equal opportunity to vote and to have their votes counted. . . .

Voter registration problems typically are the largest cause of unwarranted voter disenfranchisement in the United States. Year after year, a substantial number of Americans show up at their polling places only to find that their names are not on the voter rolls, either because of a problem in the registration process or because their names have been incorrectly removed from the rolls. Others are unable to register to vote in advance of Election Day because of restrictive voter registration requirements. Although the new statewide voter registration databases mandated by HAVA [Help America Vote Act] have the potential to mitigate these problems, that potential has not been reached, and few states have adopted policies and prac-

Wendy R. Weiser and Jonah Goldman, "An Agenda for Election Reform," 2007. Reproduced by permission of The Brennan Center for Justice at NYU School of Law and The Lawyers' Committee for Civil Rights Under Law. www.brennancenter.org.

tices to use their databases to help voters. The causes of voter registration problems are multiple, and they have been fleshed out through extensive study and advocacy experience.

Any reform agenda should address the myriad barriers to voter registration that currently plague our electoral system. Since new barriers frequently arise, a reform agenda should also include protections to ensure that additional barriers do not disenfranchise voters. And since existing voter registration systems themselves are often a significant barrier to voting for many citizens, even when they function properly, a reform agenda should seek to expand the ways in which citizens can become registered to vote. Overall, the goals of federal reform of the voter registration process are: (a) to expand the avenues for voter registration; (b) to remove technical and other barriers to voter registration; (c) to improve practices for purging the voter rolls of ineligible voters by increasing public transparency and reducing the likelihood that eligible voters will be disenfranchised; and (d) to make it easier for citizens to determine their voter registration status. . . .

---

*Congress should pass comprehensive legislation mandating necessary security protections for all voting systems.*

---

## Improve Voting Systems

Research shows that all of the most commonly purchased electronic voting systems have significant security and reliability vulnerabilities. For example, radio frequency wireless components in voting machines pose an especially large security risk, as does the failure of states to audit voter-verified paper records. Unless adequate protections are put in place, there is a risk that these voting systems could be tampered with so as to change the outcomes of elections. This risk further undermines Americans' confidence in our electoral system.

In addition to security and reliability problems, some voting systems have significant usability and accessibility problems that lead to the loss of votes. It is essential that, in making any reforms, Congress preserve the gains that HAVA made in ensuring that all voters, including voters with disabilities and language minority voters, have an opportunity to cast an independent and secret ballot. Those protections need not be compromised to ensure that new voting systems are secure and reliable.

---

*In nearly every election cycle many voters, disproportionately those in minority communities, are confronted with deceptive [voting] information.*

---

Congress should pass comprehensive legislation mandating necessary security protections for all voting systems. Congress should also take additional steps to ensure that voting systems are usable and accessible. . . .

## Prevent Disenfranchisement

*Prohibit Deceptive Practices and Voter Intimidation*

Every election cycle, voters are inundated with a flurry of information aimed at educating them about issues, candidates, and the electoral process. Unfortunately, not all of this information is designed to help voters make informed political choices; instead, in nearly every election cycle many voters, disproportionately those in minority communities, are confronted with deceptive information designed to prevent them from casting a meaningful ballot. In 2004, for example, fliers in African American neighborhoods of Milwaukee, Wisconsin falsely warned voters that if they had not paid their parking tickets, if they had ever been convicted of a felony or if they had ever voted in an election that year that they would be punished for going to the polls. In 2006, fliers distributed to voters with Latino surnames in Orange County, California incorrectly intimated that it is illegal for naturalized citizens to vote. In Virginia, Colorado and New Mexico, voters received automated calls communicating incorrect information about where and when to vote and the requirements for voting.

Congress should pass legislation that prohibits and provides voters with adequate recourse for conduct aimed at preventing them from voting through intimidating or deceptive practices. This legislation should preserve the fundamental First Amendment freedom of speech, particularly in the political arena. In addition, the legislation should include a remedial structure that provides members of affected communities with immediate, correct information from a reliable and trusted source.

### Documentation Requirements

A wave of restrictive voter ID and proof of citizenship laws and proposed laws across the country seek to condition the right to vote on presentation of a strictly limited set of documents. Tens of millions of eligible citizens do not have the documents required under those proposals, especially people of color, low-income citizens, the elderly, and students. A recent study by the Brennan Center, for example, shows that more than half of all voting-eligible women do not have proof of citizenship with their current names on it. A 2005 Wisconsin study showed that 78% of African-American men between the ages of 18 and 24 do not have driver's licenses.

In 2006, new voter ID requirements caused enormous problems and disenfranchised many across the country, even where restrictive laws were not in effect. Most notoriously, South Carolina Governor Mark Sanford and Ohio Representative Steven Chabot were turned away from the polls for lack of proper ID, and Missouri's chief election official, Robin Carnahan, was improperly asked to show photo ID despite the fact that the state's supreme court had struck down Missouri's photo ID law. Equally problematic, calls to voter protection hotlines revealed that many voters were turned away across the country even though they showed military IDs or because their addresses on their photo IDs were not current. . . .

- *Resist restrictive ID and proof of citizenship requirements.* First and foremost, Congress should resist any attempt to make proof of citizenship or photo ID a precondition of voting. Congress should similarly resist efforts to require voters to present a durable voter registration card, since a substantial number of Americans in states that currently produce such cards do not receive their cards in the mail or lose them before the election.

- *Repeal onerous provision of REAL ID Act.* The REAL ID Act of 2005, which [went] into effect in 2008, imposes a series of burdensome federal requirements on state photo ID cards, including driver's licenses. Among those is a requirement that each citizen show documentary proof of citizenship and that the state verify that documentation with the Department of Homeland Security before the individual is issued a driver's license or other photo ID. The National Governors Association, the National Council of State Legislatures, and the American Association of Motor Vehicle Administrators have estimated that it will cost states at least $11 billion to implement the REAL ID Act over the first 5 years. Because states cannot and will not comply with its mandates, and because individuals will be injured, Congress should repeal the onerous requirements of the REAL ID Act.

- *Resources for voter education on ID.* Congress should provide resources for state and local election officials to educate their voters and poll workers about what identification is necessary in order to vote as well as what identification is not required. Congress should amend Section 302 of HAVA to require that states post at every polling place, information about voter identification including what identification is required to receive a ballot.

- *Prohibit onerous state documentation requirements.* Congress should also enact protections to guard against voter disenfranchisement as a result of restrictive state-imposed voter ID or proof of citizenship requirements and the improper implementation of any such requirements.

*Ensure Fair and Effective Provisional Balloting*

Provisional balloting was one of the centerpieces of HAVA, intended to provide a fail-safe mechanism to ensure that eligible voters will not be disenfranchised as a result of administrative errors. Although provisional ballots have saved many votes that otherwise would have been lost, their promise has been severely hampered by the failure of states to adopt procedures to ensure that provisional ballots are a true fail-safe for eligible voters. Worse yet, a number of states have adopted provisional balloting procedures under which voters are provided ballots that will not be counted under any circumstances. These "placebo ballots" not only fail to provide a fail-safe for eligible voters, but they also mislead voters into believing that they have cast meaningful ballots when they have not. The problems are compounded by the fact that many states do not have uniform rules for counting provisional ballots, which means that one county might count certain provisional ballots that neighboring counties will reject.

We therefore recommend the following proposals to restore the promise of provisional ballots:

- *Require provisional ballot forms to be used as voter registration forms.* All states should be required to add eligible voters who voted by provisional ballot to their voter registration lists. The provisional ballot envelope typically includes all information required on a voter registration form. This has been implemented successfully in a number of states.

- *Uniform and transparent counting standards.* All states should be required to publish uniform and transparent standards for determining when a provisional ballot will count, well in advance of an election.

- *Provisional ballots cast by voters sent to the wrong precinct or polling place.* States should not refuse to count a provisional ballot cast by an eligible voter in the wrong precinct or polling place for all the races for which that voter was eligible to vote. This would not prevent states from maintaining a precinct-based voting system or from penalizing voters or others for deliberately undermining that system without good cause.

## Improve Election Administration

### Prevent Conflicts of Interest

Over the past few election cycles, Americans have become frustrated with election officials who seem more interested in partisan electoral successes than in ensuring that voters in their jurisdictions have the ability to cast meaningful ballots. In 2000 and 2004, the national spotlight shone on chief election officials in several states because of the conflicts of interest between their roles in running elections and their official positions in partisan political campaigns. Controversies arose over last-minute election administration decisions in those states because those decisions appeared to benefit the candidates for whom those officials were working. Regardless of whether state election officials who hold positions in partisan political campaigns actually base their election administration decisions on illegitimate partisan considerations, conflicts of interest create incentives for wrongdoing and cause voters to doubt the impartiality of those running their elections, undermining the integrity of the process. Voters should be confident that those who are selected to run their elections have the interest of democracy, and not the interest of partisanship, as their primary concern. To increase confidence in the fairness of elections, we recommend the following reforms:

- *Prevent conflicts of interest.* Congress should adopt legislation that prevents conflicts of interest by amending Title III of the Federal Election Campaign Act to prohibit chief state election officials from actively campaigning for a candidate for political office or serving as an official on a candidate's campaign.

- *Prohibit last-minute changes in election rules.* Congress should prohibit last-minute changes in the rules that govern elections. Instead, states should be required to publicly post election laws and regulations 90 days before an election and should be prevented from changing the rules after that date, except in response to court rulings or an unforeseen emergency.

*Ensure Adequate and Equitable Allocation of Election Resources*

In the past two federal election cycles, voters across the country were disenfranchised by long lines at the polling place. In 2004, for example, some voters in urban districts in Columbus, Ohio waited to vote in the pouring rain for over 5 hours while other voters in suburban precincts in the same county quickly cast ballots at their polling places. In 2006, voters in St. Louis reported similar delays at the polling place to the Election Protection hotline. It is a constant struggle for state and local election officials across the country to ensure adequate and equitable allocation of election resources, including voting machines and poll workers. These problems disproportionately affect voters who have work, family or other considerations that prevent them from spending hours at the polling place on Election Day.

- *EAC study and guidance.* Congress should require the Election Assistance Commission to study the issue of election resource allocation and develop recommendations on the most effective formula for states and local election officials to follow in making election resource allocation decisions. It should provide adequate resources for this task.

- *State plans.* Congress should require each state to submit a written plan about how it intends to adequately ensure, to the extent possible, equitable wait times for all polling places within each jurisdiction and that no voter has to wait more than one hour.

*Improve Poll Worker Recruitment and Training*

According to the Election Assistance Commission, two million poll workers are needed to run an effective federal election. Those Americans who devote their time to serve as poll workers should be praised for their commitment to our nation's democratic principles. Unfortunately, each election many polling places have too few poll workers to administer orderly and well-run elections. Equally problematic, the poll workers who do commit their time are frequently unfamiliar with essential rules and procedures. . . .

Congress should do all it can to address the problems that voters face due to a lack of poll workers or because poll workers are under-trained and under-prepared. . . .

*Enhance Information Collection and Reporting*

Although state election officials have access to useful information about voters, elections, and the electoral process, too little of that information is compiled and disseminated to the public. Better data about each election could provide a much better understanding of what works and does not work in election administration, which practices should serve as models for other jurisdictions, where problems occur, and the needs of voters in different communities, among other things.

This data should be compiled on a regular basis because both the American public and state elections systems continue to change. . . .

### Improve Voter Education

One of the most frequent causes of voter disenfranchisement is a lack of information. As our election system continues to change, voters often show up at the polling place to find new and confusing procedures and equipment. The drafters of HAVA were correct in emphasizing the responsibility of election officials to educate their constituents on how to cast a meaningful ballot. Voters need clear information about how the registration process works and what the qualifications to vote are. They should also know what to expect when they show up at the polling place. Rules about what voters cannot do, or what constitutes election fraud and intimidation, should also be clear and the penalties communicated to deter those who would like to unfairly manipulate the system. In addition, voter education programs are far less effective if they are not conveyed in a way that is accessible to the audience. Different communities respond to different messages and methods. Significant resources and attention are thus needed to improve voter education. . . .

### Encourage Electoral Innovation

Many citizens have work, family, or other obligations that make it difficult for them to participate in elections. Innovative new voting procedures could make it easier for those citizens to participate and increase voter turnout. Many states have been experimenting with new ways to vote in an attempt to increase access to the franchise. These new methods include expanded opportunities for absentee voting; opportunities for voters to vote early and in person; opportunities for voters to vote by mail; and vote centers or mega-polling places that seek to address problems created by precinct distinctions and poll worker shortages. . . .

Congress should encourage innovation in the electoral process by amending Title II of HAVA and providing the resources and direction for the EAC to study new methods of voting, including vote by mail, universal absentee voting, permanent absentee voting, early voting, vote centers, and Internet voting. . . .

## Expand the Franchise

*Restore Voting Rights to People with Past Felony Convictions*

Voting is both a fundamental right and a civic duty. Yet, alone among modern democracies, the United States permits laws that lock people out of the voting booth for life once they have been convicted of crimes. These laws are often a remnant of Jim Crow. Restoring the right to vote strengthens democracy by increasing voter participation. Political participation also helps people reintegrate into the community after serving time in prison. And re-enfranchisement means that the home communities of those convicted regain their political voice and the ability to elect representatives.

An estimated 5.3 million Americans are barred from voting because of a felony conviction. Approximately 4 million of the disenfranchised are living in our communities, working, paying taxes, and raising families; 2 million are people who have completed their sentences but remain relegated to permanent second-class citizenship. About 1.4 million African-American men are barred from voting under these laws. Their 13% disenfranchisement rate is seven times the national average. In six states, more than one in four African-American men are permanently disenfranchised.

There is a growing movement in the states—including Rhode Island, Iowa, Florida, Connecticut, Nebraska, and Alabama—to reform restrictive felony disenfranchisement laws. Congress should join this movement to halt this continuing injustice. . . .

*Ensure Voting Rights for Residents of the District of Columbia*

More than half a million Americans living in the District of Columbia currently have no right to vote in any congressional elections. As a result, those Americans have no representation in either the U.S. Senate or the House of Representatives, and they have no say over a range of matters that affect their lives, from taxes, to military service, to health care, to education, to voting rights. Congress should address this injustice and eliminate second-class citizenship for DC residents.

- Congress should pass legislation to ensure that American citizens living in the District of Columbia have voting representation in Congress.

# Organizations to Contact

*The editors have compiled the following list of organizations concerned with the issues debated in this book. The descriptions are derived from materials provided by the organizations. All have publications or information available for interested readers. The list was compiled on the date of publication of the present volume; names, addresses, and phone numbers may change. Be aware that many organizations take several weeks or longer to respond to inquiries, so allow as much time as possible.*

**Brennan Center for Justice**
New York University School of Law
161 Avenue of the Americas, 12th Floor
New York, NY   10013
(212) 998-6730 • fax: (212) 995-4550
e-mail: brennancenter@nyu.edu
Web site: www.brennancenter.org

The Brennan Center for Justice is a nonpartisan public policy and law institute that focuses on fundamental issues of democracy and justice. One part of the center's work involves advocacy for voting rights and federal election reform. The center's Federal Election Reform section tracks election reform activity at the federal level, including legislation, news, and research. Its Web site includes links to news articles, reports and other publications, and other Web pages on this issue. Its recent publications include *Universal Voter Registration Policy Summary* and *An Agenda for Election Reform.*

**Common Cause**
133 Nineteenth Street NW, 9th Floor, Washington, DC   20036
(202) 833-1200
Web site: www.commoncause.org

Common Cause is a nonpartisan nonprofit advocacy organization founded in 1970 by John Gardner as a vehicle for citizens to make their voices heard in the political process and to hold their elected leaders accountable to the public interest. The group's Election Reform Topic Center has a broad goal of overhauling the nation's system of voting, with a focus on promoting issues such as voter-verified paper ballots, election day registration, early and no-excuse absentee voting, voting by mail, and criminalization of voter suppression and intimidation tactics, among others. Its Web site is a source of information on these and other election-related issues. Its recent publications include *Voting in 2008: Ten Swing States* and *Deceptive Practices 2.0.*

## Fair Election Legal Network (FELN)

1730 Rhode Island Ave. NW, Suite 712
Washington, DC   20036
(202) 331-0114 • fax: (202) 331-1663
e-mail: admin@fairelectionsnetwork.com
Web site: www.fairelectionsnetwork.com

The Fair Elections Legal Network is a national nonpartisan network of private and organizational election lawyers who work to remove legal impediments to voter participation and to promote laws or administrative decisions that grant broader participation in voting. FELN's Web site contains news articles and information about state legislative developments affecting the nation's elections system.

## Fair Vote

6930 Carroll Ave., Suite 610, Takoma Park, MD   20910
(301) 270-4616 • fax: (301) 270-4133
e-mail: info@fairvote.org
Web site: www.fairvote.org

Fair Vote, founded in 1992, operated for many years as the Center for Voting and Democracy. Fair Vote works to achieve universal access to election participation, a full spectrum of meaningful ballot choices, and majority rule with fair representation for all. The group promotes issues such as a constitutionally protected right to vote, universal voter registration, a national popular vote for president, instant runoff voting, and proportional representation. Fair Vote's Web site contains links to research reports, policy documents, and a periodic newsletter. Its recent publications include *A Survey and Analysis of Statewide Election Recounts, 1980–2006* and *Uniformity in Election Administration: A 2008 Survey of Swing State County Clerks.*

## Federal Election Commission (FEC)

999 E Street NW, Washington, DC   20463
(800) 424-9530
Web site: www.fec.gov

Congress created the Federal Election Commission as an independent regulatory agency in 1975 to administer and enforce the Federal Election Campaign Act (FECA)—the statute that governs the financing of federal elections. The duties of the FEC are to disclose campaign finance information, to enforce the provisions of the law such as the limits and prohibitions on contributions, and to oversee the public funding of presidential elections. Its Web site provides information about campaign finance issues and the laws and regulations governing this matter.

## Lawyers' Committee for Civil Rights Under Law

1401 New York Ave. NW, Suite 400, Washington, DC   20005
(202) 662-8315 • fax: (202) 783-5130
e-mail: jgreenbaum@lawyerscomm.org
Web site: www.lawyerscomm.org

For four decades, the Lawyers' Committee for Civil Rights Under Law has been at the forefront of the legal struggle to secure racial justice and equal access to the electoral process for all voters. Its Voting Rights Project is an integrated program of litigation, advocacy, and education that, with the help of private law firms, seeks to promote fairness and equality in elections. The project's Web site is a source of election-related news, reports, and litigation updates.

## National Commission on Federal Election Reform
c/o ReformElections.org, The Century Foundation
41 E. Seventieth Street, New York, NY   10021
(212) 535-4441
e-mail: info@tcf.org
Web site: www.reformelections.org/ncfer.asp

The National Commission on Federal Election Reform comprises public leaders from across the political spectrum. It was formed in the wake of the 2000 election crisis to quickly evaluate research on election reform, review policy proposals, and offer a bipartisan analysis to Congress, the administration, and the American people. Between March and June 2001, the commission held four public hearings and organized task forces on the federal election system, election administration, and constitutional and federal election law issues. The commission released its final report to Congress and the White House on July 31, 2001. In response, the bipartisan Help America Vote Act (HAVA) was passed in 2002 by Congress and signed into law by President George W. Bush. The commission's report, news reports, task force reports, and hearing testimony are available at its Web site.

## National Voting Rights Institute (NVRI)
27 School Street, Suite 500, Boston, MA   02108
(617) 624-3900 • fax: (617) 624-3911
e-mail: nvri@nvri.org
Web site: www.nvri.org

The National Voting Rights Institute is a nonpartisan, nonprofit organization committed to making real the promise of American democracy, that meaningful political participation and power should be accessible to all regardless of economic or social status. NVRI's goals are to promote reforms that limit campaign spending, strengthen political participation, support the constitutional protection of the right to vote, and obtain public funding for local, state, and federal elections. The NVRI Web site contains links to news articles, opinion pieces, and reports of NVRI activities.

## Pew Center on the States (PCS)

901 E Street NW, 10th Floor, Washington, DC   20004-1409
(202) 552-2000 • fax: (202) 552-2299
e-mail: statepolicymail@pewtrusts.org
Web site: www.pewcenteronthestates.org

Part of the Pew Charitable Trusts, the Pew Center on the States works to advance state policies that serve the public interest in areas such as elections, government performance, corrections, and education. It conducts credible research, brings together diverse perspectives, analyzes states' experiences to determine what works and what does not, and advances nonpartisan, pragmatic solutions for pressing problems affecting Americans. One PCS project, Make Voting Work, was launched in January 2007 and seeks to foster an election system that achieves the highest standards of accuracy, convenience for eligible voters, efficiency, and security. Electionline.org, a part of the Make Voting Work initiative, is a Web site that provides up-to-the-minute news and analysis about election reform. PCS is a source of numerous reports about election issues, including *Data for Democracy* and *Help America Vote Act at 5.*

## ReformElections.org

c/o The Century Foundation, 41 E. Seventieth Street
New York, NY   10021
(212) 535-4441
e-mail: info@tcf.org
Web site: www.reformelections.org

ReformElections.org is an informational Web site on election reform policy maintained by The Century Foundation, a nonprofit public policy research institution that has been at the forefront of efforts to reform the voting system since the issue achieved national prominence following the 2000 presidential contest. In addition to ongoing research on election reform issues, ReformElections.org features resource guides, policy developments, and the latest research from the election reform community.

## United States Election Assistance Commission (EAC)
1225 New York Ave., Suite 1100, Washington, DC   20005
(866) 747-1471
Web site: www.eac.gov

The U.S. Election Assistance Commission, established by the Help America Vote Act of 2002 (HAVA), is an independent bipartisan commission charged with developing guidance to meet HAVA requirements, adopting voluntary voting system guidelines, and serving as a national clearinghouse of information about election administration. EAC also accredits testing laboratories and certifies voting systems, as well as audits the use of HAVA funds. The EAC Web site provides information for voters, for elections officials, and contains EAC-commissioned publications such as *The Electoral College* and *Alternative Voting Methods Study*.

## USA.gov
Office of Citizen Services and Communications
U.S. General Services Administration, Washington, DC   20405
(800) 333-4636
Web site: www.usa.gov

USA.gov is the federal government's official Web portal. Under the topic Voting and Elections, visitors can access a wealth of information about federal elections, the electoral college, registering to vote and voting, voting legislation and reform, contacting elected officials, volunteering as poll workers, and campaign finance laws. The site also contains educational materials for teachers and students.

# Bibliography

## Books

| | |
|---|---|
| R. Michael Alvarez and Thad E. Hall | *Electronic Elections: The Perils and Promises of Digital Democracy.* Princeton, NJ: Princeton University Press, 2008. |
| R. Michael Alvarez, Thad E. Hall, and Susan D. Hyde | *Election Fraud: Detecting and Deterring Electoral Manipulation.* Washington, DC: Brookings Institution Press, 2008. |
| Bruce E. Cain, Todd Donovan, and Caroline J. Tolbert | *Democracy in the States: Experiments in Election Reform.* Washington, DC: Brookings Institution Press, 2008. |
| Tracy Campbell | *Deliver the Vote: A History of Election Fraud, an American Political Tradition, 1742–2004.* New York: Basic Books, 2006. |
| Steve Freeman and Joel Bleifuss | *Was the 2004 Presidential Election Stolen? Exit Polls, Election Fraud, and the Official Count.* New York: Seven Stories, 2006. |
| John Fund | *Stealing Elections: How Voter Fraud Threatens Our Democracy.* Revised and Updated. New York: Encounter Books, 2008. |

| Paul S. Herrnson, Richard G. Niemi, Michael J. Hanmer, and Benjamin B. Bederson | *Voting Technology: The Not-So-Simple Act of Casting a Ballot.* Washington, DC: Brookings Institution Press, 2008. |
| --- | --- |
| Michael J. Malbin | *The Election After Reform: Money, Politics, and the Bipartisan Campaign Reform Act.* Lanham, MD: Rowman & Littlefield, 2006. |
| Mark Crispin Miller | *Loser Take All: Election Fraud and the Subversion of Democracy, 2000–2008.* New York: Ig, 2008. |
| David W. Moore | *How to Steal an Election: The Inside Story of How George Bush's Brother and FOX Network Miscalled the 2000 Election and Changed the Course of History.* New York: Nation Books, 2006. |
| Michael Nelson | *The Elections of 2008.* Washington, DC: CQ Press, 2009. |
| Greg Palast | *Armed Madhouse: Who's Afraid of Osama Wolf? The Best Legal Whorehouse in Texas, the Scheme to Steal Election '08, No Child's Behind Left, and Other Investigations.* New York: Dutton, 2007. |
| Greg Palast | *The Best Democracy Money Can Buy.* New York: Plume, 2004. |

William Poundstone — *Gaming the Vote: Why Elections Aren't Fair (and What We Can Do About It).* New York: Hill and Wang, 2009.

Allen Raymond and Ian Spiegelman — *How to Rig an Election: Confessions of a Republican Operative.* New York: Simon & Schuster, 2008.

Frederic Charles Schaffer — *The Hidden Costs of Clean Election Reform.* Ithaca, NY: Cornell University Press, 2008.

Rodney A. Smith — *Money, Power, and Elections: How Campaign Finance Reform Subverts American Democracy.* Baton Rouge: Louisiana State University Press, 2006.

## Periodicals

*Atlanta Journal-Constitution* — "Electoral College: The Real Deciders," November 3, 2008. www.ajc.com/services/content/news/stories/2008/11/03/pecollege.html.

Association for Computing Machinery — "ACM Experts See Some Progress, but Reiterate Need to Improve US Election System Technology," November 13, 2008. www.acm.org/press-room/news-releases-2008/evoting-election08/.

Anne E. Baker            "Help America Vote Act: A
                         Misnomer?" Paper delivered at the
                         2007 annual meeting of the
                         American Political Science
                         Association, August 30–September 2,
                         2007. www.allacademic.com//
                         meta/p_mla_apa_research_citation/
                         2/1/1/7/1/pages211718/p211718-1.php.

Joel Barkin              "End the 'Voter Fraud' Debate,"
and Christian            *Nation*, October 31, 2008.
Smith-Socaris            www.thenation.com/doc/20081117/
                         barkin_smith.

Marc Caplan              "New Openings for Public
                         Financing," *American Prospect*,
                         October 22, 2007. www.prospect.org/
                         cs/articles?article=new_openings_for
                         _public_financing.

Liz Colville             "Facets of the U.S. Election: The
                         Voting Booth," *Finding Dulcinea*,
                         January 8, 2008.
                         www.findingdulcinea.com/features/
                         feature-articles/facets-of-the-us-
                         presidential-election/The-Voting-Booth.html.

Michael Cooper           "A Landslide Election? No, but a
                         Clear Win, for a Change,"
                         *International Herald-Tribune*,
                         November 7, 2008. www.iht.com/
                         articles/2008/11/07/america/07elect.php.

Christopher Drew          "Overhaul Plan for Voting System
                         Will Be Delayed," *New York Times*,
                         July 20, 2007. www.nytimes.com/
                         2007/07/20/washington/20vote.html.

| Daphne Eviatar | "Election 2008: The Voting Problems Aren't Over," *AmLaw Daily*, November 11, 2008. http://amlawdaily.typepad.com/ amlawdaily/2008/11/election-2008-t.html. |

| Daya Gamage | "Credibility of US Presidential Election a Big Issue," *Asian Tribune*, October 28, 2004. www.asiantribune.com/ oldsite/show_news.php?id=11833. |

| Dan Goodin | "E-voting Glitches Hamper Elections in Seven States," *Register*, November 4, 2008. www.theregister.co.uk/ 2008/11/04/election_day_evoting_glitches/. |

| Katrina vanden Heuvel | "America Needs Electoral Reform," *Nation*, July 21, 2008. www.thenation.com/doc/ 20080721/kvh. |

| Robert F. Kennedy, Jr. | "Will the Next Election Be Hacked? Fresh Disasters at the Polls—and New Evidence from an Industry Insider—Prove That Electronic Voting Machines Can't Be Trusted," *Rolling Stone*, October 2008. www.rollingstone.com/politics/ story/11717105/robert_f_kennedy_ jr_will_the_next_election_be_hacked. |

Robert F. Kennedy, Jr. and Greg Palast
"Block the Vote: Will the GOP's Campaign to Deter New Voters and Discard Democratic Ballots Determine the Next President?" *Rolling Stone*, October 30, 2008. www.rollingstone.com/politics/ story/23638322/block_the_vote.

Michelle Mairesse
"How American Elections Became a Criminal Enterprise," *Hermes Press*, February 23, 2006. www.hermes-press.com/ criminal_vote.htm.

Thomas E. Mann
"Money in the 2008 Elections: Bad News or Good?" *Chautauquan Daily*, July 1, 2008. Reprinted at www.brookings.edu/opinions/ 2008/0701_publicfinance_mann.aspx.

*New York Times*
"Still Broken," March 17, 2009. www.nytimes.com/2009/03/18/ opinion/18wed1.html?_r=1.

Greg Palast
"How They Stole the Mid-Term Election," *Global Research*, November 7, 2006. www.globalresearch.ca/ index.php?context=va&aid=3757.

*Philadelphia Inquirer*
"Electronic Voting Machines," editorial, February 28, 2009. www.philly.com/inquirer/ opinion/20090228_Editorial_ Electronic_Voting_Machines.html.

William          "A Paper Trail for Voting Machines,"
Poundstone       *New York Times*, January 7 2008.
                 www.nytimes.com/2008/01/07/
                 opinion/07poundstone.html.

Karl Rove        "McCain Couldn't Compete with
                 Obama's Money," *Wall Street Journal*,
                 December 4, 2008.
                 http://online.wsj.com/article/
                 SB122835139848377873.html.

Christian Smith  "How Our Election Systems Held Up
                 Under a High Turnout Election,"
                 *Progressive States Network*, November
                 14, 2008. www.progressivestates.org/
                 node/22408.

Clive Thompson   "Can You Count on Voting
                 Machines?" *New York Times
                 Magazine*, January 6, 2008.
                 www.nytimes.com/2008/01/06/
                 magazine/06Vote-t.html?_r=2
                 &ref=magazine&oref=slogin.

Ian Urbina       "Hurdles to Voting Persisted in
                 2008," *New York Times*, March 10,
                 2009. www.nytimes.com/2009/03/11/
                 us/politics/11vote.html?_r=1.

U.S. General     "Elections: Federal Efforts to Improve
Accounting Office Security and Reliability of Electronic
                 Voting Systems Are Under Way, but
                 Key Activities Need to Be
                 Completed," September 21, 2005.
                 www.gao.gov/products/GAO-05-956.

Kim Zetter        "Election Problems Around the
Country," *Wired*, November 04, 2008.
http://blog.wired.com/27bstroke6/2008/
11/election-prob-1.html.

# Index